Anindita Balslev, Dirk Evers (Eds.)

Compassion in the World's Religions

Compassion
in the World's Religions

Envisioning Human Solidarity

edited by

Anindita Balslev and Dirk Evers

LIT

Bibliographic information published by the Deutsche Nationalbibliothek
The Deutsche Nationalbibliothek lists this publication in the Deutsche
Nationalbibliografie; detailed bibliographic data are available in the Internet at
http://dnb.d-nb.de.

ISBN 978-3-643-10476-2

A catalogue record for this book is available from the British Library

©LIT VERLAG Dr. W. Hopf Berlin 2010
Fresnostr. 2   D-48159 Münster
Tel. +49 (0) 2 51-620 32 22   Fax +49 (0) 2 51-922 60 99
e-Mail: lit@lit-verlag.de   http://www.lit-verlag.de

Distribution:
In Germany: LIT Verlag Fresnostr. 2, D-48159 Münster
Tel. +49 (0) 2 51-620 32 22, Fax +49 (0) 2 51-922 60 99, e-Mail: vertrieb@lit-verlag.de

In Austria: Medienlogistik Pichler-ÖBZ GmbH & Co KG
IZ-NÖ, Süd, Straße 1, Objekt 34, A-2355 Wiener Neudorf
Tel. +43 (0) 22 36-63 53 52 90, Fax +43 (0) 22 36-63 53 52 43, e-Mail: mlo@medien-logistik.at

In Switzerland: B + M Buch- und Medienvertriebs AG
Hochstr. 357, CH-8200 Schaffhausen
Tel. +41 (0) 52-643 54 30, Fax +41 (0) 52-643 54 35, e-Mail: order@buch-medien.ch

In the UK by: Global Book Marketing, 99B Wallis Rd, London, E9 5LN
Phone: +44 (0) 20 8533 5800 – Fax: +44 (0) 1600 775 663
http://www.centralbooks.co.uk/html

In North America by:

Transaction Publishers
New Brunswick (U.S.A.) and London (U.K.)

Transaction Publishers
Rutgers University
35 Berrue Circle
Piscataway, NJ 08854

Phone: +1 (732) 445 - 2280
Fax: + 1 (732) 445 - 3138
for orders (U. S. only):
toll free (888) 999 - 6778
e-mail: orders@transactionpub.com

Foreword

Compassion, or 'Karuna' in the Hindu tradition, is considered to be one of the cardinal virtues. The Ramayana, for example, was born when Rishi Valmiki spontaneously broke into a new metre out of compassion at seeing a hunter shoot dead one of a pair of Kraunch birds making love. Indeed all the world's great religions deify compassion. Lord Shiva is described as 'Karunavataram', the incarnation of compassion, while the Holy Quran describes Allah as compassionate and merciful. Christ's compassion for suffering humanity led him to the Cross, while it impelled Prince Siddhartha to leave his palatial home and seek an end to suffering.

The problem arises when we revere compassion but do not practice it in our actions. There has been so much cruelty by all religions; notice the Spanish Inquisition and the so-called Islamist Jehadis! Any project, therefore, which seeks to bring together representatives of the world's religions in a creative dialogue revolving around the concept of compassion, is to be welcomed.

The whole Interfaith movement revolves around the basic concept of multiple paths to the Divine. From 1893 when the first Parliament of World Religions was held in Chicago, through the 20th century a.d. during which a wide spectrum of Interfaith organizations came into existence including the Temple of Understanding with which I have been closely associated for several decades, down to the fifth Parliament in Melbourne in December 2009. The whole attempt has been to encourage a positive, concept oriented dialogue between representatives of the great religious traditions of the world, and to encourage friendship and solidarity rather than conflict and confrontation.

My warm commendation to the Editors of this volume and Organizers of the conferences on Human Solidarity and Compassion Anindita N. Balslev and Dirk Evers.

Karan Singh

Editorials

Whenever even a small part of a big dream turns into reality, it brings with it a sense of hope. Our hope is to continue with the endeavor that can be of some help for discerning and construing common values across cultures and traditions.

It is a decade ago that I was invited to an international conference on the 'Great Religions of Asia'. I took that occasion to discuss about some of the conceptual overlaps in the philosophical formulations of the notion of compassion in the Upanisadic and the Buddhist traditions, despite the metaphysical differences that have earned these traditions the nomenclatures of Atmavada and Anatmavada. I remarked in the course of my presentation that "it is regrettable that an authentic encounter of world-religions has not happened in a manner that could show us clearly in what sense and with what intent a common path is taken in the sphere of value-orientation, highlighting this great idea of compassion or Karuna".

I am truly grateful that this dream of bringing traditions together has begun to realise, first when Dirk Evers and I held a small meeting in Neversdorf, Germany in 2008 and then in a somewhat larger way as part of the CCC international conference that I organized in New Delhi in January 2009, focusing on the theme of 'Human Solidarity: Visions and Projects'. Among others, several scholars from different religious traditions were invited precisely with the view of exploring the idea of compassion along with its practical implications. This volume consists of papers that were presented on that occasion. We are now heading for the auspicious event of the Parliament of World's Religions where we are planning to discuss both cognitive and practical aspects of the idea of compassion in the contemporary context of a range of crisis. It seems to us that repeated attempt to stimulate the collective will is necessary so that we may eventually grasp the most vital messages of the religions of the world.

We ask for the readers' compassion for all the limitations that this volume has. It is quickly compiled with the intention of making the work available during the upcoming event of the Parliament of the World's Religions to be held in Melbourne in December 2009. Although the editors are aware that these papers are contributed by scholars who have deep knowledge of their own traditions, nonetheless for many of the contributors English is not only not their first language, it is also not a medium of their daily exchanges. Given the short time available to us, it has not been possible for us to edit the papers presented or to put in place the diacritical marks on Sanskrit words or to correct other shortcomings. We will consider our effort to be worthwhile if these papers can convey the spirit of the undertaking and the readers appreciate it as an honest venture to cross 'hard boundaries' with the view of enriching the discourse concerning common values in a global context.

We believe that the world-religions are the primary source of values and that by focusing on a value like compassion we can actually close the wide gap that is usually taken to exist among the world's religions. Let this work be seen as an attempt to remind us all that we can do something to alter the perception so aptly expressed by Jonathan Swift: "We have enough religions to hate one another but not enough to love one another".

However, what is of our foremost concern here is to underscore that compassion is not just a fleeting sentiment but a shared value, that when translated into practice it shows itself as a transformative force that can reduce and eventually eliminate all man-made suffering that vitiate our collective life. The religions of the world insist that the practice of compassion not only transforms the lives of the recipients of compassion but also those of the practitioners themselves and that too in a manner so that the conflicting pulls of 'good of one', 'good of few' and 'good of all' cease to exist. These teachings emphasizing the 'unity of all beings' can surely provide one of the strongest impetus for fostering a sense of human solidarity.

Let me thank the India Habitat Center, the Indian Council of World Affairs, New Delhi for supporting the CCC conference held in New Delhi in the beginning of this year. However, support received from the Udo Keller Foundation has been vital for this entire endeavor, starting from the Neversdorf meeting leading to the Parliament of the World's Religions as well as for this publication. Our sincere thanks to all these organizations, to the contributors and to the audience!

India, November 2009   Anindita N. Balslev

****

Religion is one of the most intimate and intense influences on human beings, deeply related to the formation of their individual, personal identities. At the same time, the presence of the divine, of religious fulfilment
and happiness, transcends the individual selves. It transcends borders of
social and class differences, of gender, age and nationality. It nourishes
love toward other human beings and even beyond humanity, and this love
is rooted in the deep identity between us and the others. And it is a well
known fact that a notion of compassion, of a deeply felt responsibility for
and move toward the fellow being, especially to the poor, deprived, helpless and needy fellow being is at the centre of many religious ethics. Thus
religion is able to bring about, cultivate and obtain communities with a
deep sense of solidarity.

But then again, precisely by transgressing natural divisions between
human beings, religions also tend to establish new borders, religiously justified distinctions of class, cast and status, of 'we' and 'the others', of holy
and unholy, of innocence and well-deserved punishment. And politics can
easily exploit these religious divides. In a globalised world, this has become
a challenge to the concepts of compassion and solidarity propagated by the
world's religions. How can believers, how can followers of a religious path
bring about, cultivate and obtain forms of compassion and human solidarity which are relevant to a globalised world – a world shaken by poverty
and injustice and ruled by technical, economical and monetary imperatives
which apparently do not allow for mutual care and concerns?

In two conferences, the first held as an intense workshop at the beautifully located house of the Udo Keller Foundation – Forum Humanum in
Neversdorf near Hamburg, Germany, the second as a bigger public event
organised by Anindita Balslev at the Habitat Center in New Delhi, India,
scholars from different religious traditions and, in the case of the Indian
meeting, from the political sphere joined to discuss these issues of compassion and solidarity. Most of the contributions are collected in this volume
with a special emphasis on the religious traditions, involving Zoroastrism,
Buddhism, Hinduism, Judaism, Christianity and Islam.

Though we concentrated on exploring and sharing our different traditions, some overarching perspectives emerged which I find worth commu-
nicating in these editorial remarks. Five issues seemed especially relevant:

1. Compassion is both, an *instinct* and a *virtue*. It is deeply grounded in
basic human properties such as empathy and instinctive pity for the needy.

On the other hand it suffers from the ambivalence of human relationships, the tension between me and the other, between 'us' and 'them'. All religions promote a cultivation of compassion as a virtue to lead it beyond its natural resources and transform it into a life-shaping force.

2. Compassion as a virtue is promoted through *imitation* and *identification*. All religions seem to flesh our compassion both vertically and horizontally. Vertically they frame compassion as the imitation of a role model, of Jesus, the Prophet, the Buddha, of God himself in his ultimate mercy. Horizontally they provide foundations and means for identification between human beings (e.g. as children of God or the Divine). Different concepts of compassion might be compared along these lines.

3. There may be *limits of compassion*. Unlimited compassion might turn into terror for both, for the subject as well as for the object of compassion.

4. There may be no meaningful general notion of *compassion as such*. Concepts of compassion seem to be shaped relative to a certain culture and religion. The task ahead might not be to find the common denominator of compassion, but to develop a new culture of compassion in a global context.

5. Thus the *emergence of compassion* must be stimulated. Compassion is not a technique, it has to be discovered. Its emergence can be nurtured and fostered, but it cannot be technically produced. Religions promote compassion mainly through narratives, role models and character forming ritual practices, i.e. through 'lose' forms of rationality. Compassion, therefore, also needs freedom of technical imperatives in order to develop. The dissolution of the knowledge and practice of such narratives, role models and rituals poses a challenge for secular societies.

Most contributions in this volume provide starting points of exploration from within different religious traditions. It is our conviction that we will all benefit when we embark on a common journey toward compassion. Therefore, our thanks go to the Udo Keller Foundation – Forum Humanum in Neversdorf, Germany, whose generous support made both conferences possible as well as the printing of this book. The India Habitat Center was a valuable host to the conference in Delhi which was also supported by the Indian Council of World Affairs. We thank both institutions cordially for their support.

Germany, November 2009   Dirk Evers

Contents

A Short Note: Concern and Compassion as Pathways to Making Hunger History

IN THE YEAR 2000, world leaders assembling at the UN in New York resolved to reduce the number of children, women and men going to bed hungry by half by 2015. Yet the latest estimate of the Food and Agriculture Organisation of the UN on the prevalence of hunger, indicates that hunger is increasing and that over a billion go to bed hungry now, as compared to about 820 million in the year 2000. Why are we witnessing this growing gap between plans and achievement in the area of hunger elimination?

Food and drinking water are the first among the hierarchical needs of a human being. This is why Mahatma Gandhi remarked in 1946 at Naokhali (now in Bangladesh) that to the hungry, God is bread and that the first and foremost duty of independent India is to ensure that this God lives in every home and hut in the country. Unfortunately over 200 million children, women and men are undernourished in India.

The Government of India has introduced a large number of nutrition safety net programmes, starting with the Integrated Child Development Service (ICDS) for 0 to 5 year children and noon-meal programme in schools. In spite of all such schemes, hunger persists. Among the three categories of hunger – endemic hunger, (protein – calorie energy deprivation), hidden hunger caused the deficiency of micro-nutrients like Vitamin A, iron, iodine, zinc, vitamin B12, etc., and transient hunger caused by natural or man-made calamities, endemic hunger results largely from poverty. Today, hunger is not related to non-availability of food in the market. A famine of jobs, leading to the famine of purchasing power is the principal cause of hunger. Where there is income, there is food. Therefore, poverty alleviation will help in eliminating hunger.

Mahatma Gandhi emphasized that food must be available to everyone without any compromise on human dignity. In other words, *food with human dignity must be our goal.* This will call for a mind set change from patronage to partnership. Such a paradigm shift in mind-set will come only with a spirit of compassion. Compassion results in genuine concern for the hungry and makes one feel that the persistence of hunger is morally and spiritually inexcusable. Such awareness leads to analysis of the pathways to achieve freedom from hunger. Analysis finally leads to action.

Without compassion, hunger will continue to prevail. This has many adverse consequences. First, as emphasized by the Roman Philosopher Seneca, "a hungry person listens to neither reason nor religion, nor is bent by any prayers". Maternal and foetal under-nutrition leads to the birth of babies with a low birth weight (LBW), and such LBW children suffer from many handicaps including impaired cognitive ability. This is the cruellest form of inequity in this knowledge age. A compassionate mind will tell us that we have no right to deny child opportunities for the full development of his/ her innate genetic potential for physical and mental development.

A compassionate mind is a caring mind. This conference should lead to the birth of a *coalition of the compassionate.* Such a coalition can help to spread the following message beautifully expressed by W. H. Auden:

Coalition of the Compassionate

"Hunger allows no choice

To the citizen or the police;

We must love one another or die.

Defenceless under the night

Our world in stupor lies;

Yet, dotted everywhere,

Ironic points of light

Flash out wherever the Just

Exchange their messages:

May I, composed like them

Of Eros and of dust,

Beleaguered by the same

Negation and despair,

Show an affirming flame."

1. Chapter

The Zoroastrian Ethos of Compassion

Homi Dhalla

THE FOCUS OF THIS PAPER is to examine the concept of 'compassion' in the Zoroastrian tradition and the impact it has had on the lives of its adherents and others. The Zoroastrian texts graphically depict Ahura Mazda the Creator, as the 'merciful and compassionate Lord' and also the 'Forgiver of sins'. Besides being 'Loving', he is benevolent and kind towards His creation (*Menok Xrat* I.16).

All these attributes and many more, depict the nature of Ahura Mazda. It is man's duty to emulate these qualities in his day to day life so that he progresses. As progress is the Zoroastrian watchword, he is expected to move from the love of his family to the welfare of all creatures. This ethos of progress as well as inclusiveness are one of the important elements of this ancient faith. This is clearly brought out in many prayers, one of which may be cited here:

> May the waters be ever and ever flowing, the trees be ever and ever growing, the corn be ever and ever ripening. May the thoughts, words and actions of us all be truthful and righteous, so that, in the end, all of mankind may be benefited, in this world and in the other world (*Afrin-i-haft Ameshaspandan*, 15–17).

Compassion is one of the most articulate values in the Zoroastrian tradition. This spiritual value plays a significant role and which has actually been translated into action in many cases. To a Zoroastrian, this feeling of compassion is stronger than empathy. It is a deep desire to alleviate the suffering of others. This is demonstrated by a fervent prayer in the Atash Nyaish (Litany to Light). Standing before the holy Fire, which is an inspiring and dynamic symbol of Divine Light, a devotee fervently prays "Grant me a child [...] who would relieve distress" (Atash Nyaish, 5). Another ancient text, the Visparad also accentuates "Ye Zoroastrians! Hold your hands and feet in preparedness [...] Relieve those who have fallen in distress" (Visparad, XV.I). This demonstrates a great sensitivity to the suffering of all living beings irrespective of caste, colour or religion. This selfless compassion would undoubtedly lead to spiritual evolution (kindness towards animals is a recurring theme in Zoroastrian texts). Moreover, a part of the Ahunavar which is the oldest and the most important Zoroastrian prayer affirms that "He who provides succour to the helpless poor, acknowledges the kingdom of God". Prophet Zarathushtra asks Ahura Mazda, "O Mazda! What is Your kingdom? What is Your Will, by acting according to which, I may come unto Your friendship? Ahura Mazda replies: "You will come unto my friendship by helping your poor fellowmen who live righteously and with a loving mind (Yasna, 34.5).

Furthermore, one is expected to go far beyond the limits of compassion in relieving the suffering of those in distress – the *Denkard* declares that "Apart from the salvation for one's soul, it is best to strive for saving other people's soul". Hence, it is imperative to cultivate our minds and mould our actions in such a manner that we work for the liberation of others. This is a great moral and spiritual responsibility. Hence, a Zoroastrian is expected not merely to work for his own salvation but it is best for him to work for the liberation of other souls. This consciousness of compassion will help others to be liberated from suffering.

A discussion about compassion would be incomplete without examining two of the fundamental principles of Zoroastrianism, *nidhasnaithishem* (non-violence) and *khaetwadatham* (self-sacrifice or service). To a Zoroastrian, the life of every creature is sacred. Any form of violent action is unacceptable. This compassionate and non-violent attitude is to be extended even to nature as Zoroastrianism is an ecological religion. A Zoroastrian is to live in harmony with nature. Hence, he should not pollute or harm the various elements of nature thereby bringing about an imbalance.

This compassionate attitude towards nature makes him a trustee of nature and in that capacity he should not violate that trust by destroying or harming nature.

Khaetwadatham, leading a life of self-sacrifice, altruism or service to humanity is another principle which is also an extension of compassionate living. Service to our fellow brothers has been greatly emphasized in

Zoroastrian texts. Zarathushtra declares that "one who strives to understand and attain a true life, should preach the law of Ahura Mazda to mankind better by acts of service than by words" (*Yasna*, 51.19). And again he states "[...] urging the inner self to serve mankind, O Mazda, the Highest shall be reached by deeds alone, for action true I strive and ever will" (*Yasna*, 51.1). Moreover, "joy comes to the one who brings joy to others" (*Yasna*, 43.1).

Closely connected to this concept is another important ideal which is also motivated by their religious tradition – that accumulation of wealth by honest means is considered fundamentally positive. This, however, in turn brings with it a social obligation to share one's wealth with the less fortunate.

In this context, it is imperative to note that the one characteristic which is usually attributed to a Zoroastrian is his large-heartedness or philanthropy – "Parsi, thy name is charity". This is considered a sacred duty. There are several references in the scriptures, which extols this cardinal virtue; one of these is from the *Menok Xrat*, which states, "The greatest act of righteousness is charity" (*Menok Xrat* IV. 2,4). Besides this, the Prophet declares "May we be surely like those, who make this world prosperous. May the chosen leaders of Mazda be helpers and supporters of the world" (*Yasna*, 30.9). Hence, Parsi history in India is replete with examples of how this miniscule community of barely 70,000 in a burgeoning population of over a billion has been endowing schools, colleges, parks, hospitals, dharamshalas etc. for the benefit of all communities, including hospitals for animals.

I. Sharing the Fruits of Industry

Max Weber had stated that economic ethics are considered as "the practical incentives for human actions which are derived from the psychological and pragmatic dimensions of a religion". In this context, it is also pertinent to note the words of Andriano Tigher that "Zoroastrianism prized labour and gave it an ethical value". Perhaps the best example of this principle is that of Jamsetji Tata (1839–1905), the man who laid the foundation of Indian industry. Jamsetji was initiated into priesthood at a young age and hence his Zoroastrian religious tradition had influenced his character and moulded his values of deep social commitment and philanthropy.

The late Pandit Jawaharlal Nehru, the first Prime Minister of India had said, "The three fundamental requirements of India, if she is to develop industrially and otherwise are: a heavy engineering and machine-making industry, scientific research institutes and electric power. These must be the foundations of all planning". And Jamsetji provided India with all three enterprises viz., Tata Iron and Steel Co. Ltd. at Jamshedpur, Tata Power – Hydro Electric Works at Lonavla and the Indian Institute of Science at Bangalore. It is no wonder that Nehru had observed that "he was a one-man planning commission". Though a staunch Zoroastrian, his catholic spirit is evident in a letter he wrote to his son from abroad in 1902, five years before the site of the steel plant at Jamshedpur was finally located: "Be sure there is plenty of space for lawns, playgrounds [...] and parks. Earmark areas for Hindu temples, Mohammedan mosques and Christian churches". Furthermore, his commitment to the development of India was so intense that when he did not receive cooperation from the British government to set up a science university, in September 1898, he announced a personal donation of Rs. 30 lacs to launch the Indian Institute of Science at Bangalore.

Although, he was concerned with gigantic projects of national magnitude, his compassion extended even to animals. A very touching example of this trait came to light only recently. In 1900, due to the famine, millions were affected. In the small village of Chharodi (35 kms. from Ahmedabad) in Gujarat, a large number of animals were starving to death; Jamsetji had sent a donation to save these animals. This came to light in December 2008, through a marble plaque that was found on the land that his great grandson, Ratan Tata has now been given by the Government of Gujarat to set up the small car 'Nano' plant.

This compassionate streak is also visible today in the life and actions of Ratan Tata, Chairman of Tata industries. The thought which inspired Ratan to manufacture the 'Nano' the cheapest car in the world was triggered when he saw young couples driving precariously with their children on two wheelers.

On February 8, 1911, Jamsetji's son, Sir Dorabji Tata, laid the foundation stone of the Lonavla dam and thus commenced the hydroelectric project. On this occasion he recalled the lofty aims of his father by saying: "To my father, the acquisition of wealth was only a secondary object in life; it was always subordinate to the constant desire in his heart to improve the industrial and intellectual condition of the people of this country". J R D

Tata who led the Tata industrial empire for over 50 years once said: "The wealth gathered by Jamsetji Tata and his sons in half a century of industrial pioneering formed but a minute fraction of the amount by which they enriched the nation. The whole of that wealth is held in trust for the people and used exclusively for their benefit. The cycle is thus complete; what came from the people has gone back to the people, many times over". The pleasure in earning truly lies in its distribution. JRD Tata acknowledged the humanitarian nature of his religious tradition when he wrote to a friend in April 1984: "The Zoroastrian philosophy of hard work, honesty and charity is one that the world should know today".

The House of Tata has touched every aspect of Indian life through its several institutions such as the Tata Institute of Social Science, Tata Memorial Hospital for Cancer, Tata Institute of Fundamental Research, Tata Blood Bank and Transfusion Services, Tata Agricultural and Rural Training for the Blind, National Centre for Performing Arts and many others.

II. Corporate Social Responsibility of the House of Tata

R. M. Lala, author of the best-selling book on the House of Tata, The Creation of Wealth, emphasizes that wealth is far from just profit or income generation. It has deep concern with "weal which means well-being or happiness" of all members of society which businesses serve. The company's soul lies in its social involvement. And that is what the Tata Group is determined to maintain.

The panoply of community development projects launched by the Tata companies embraces everything from health, education, art, sport and more – thereby touching the lives of multitudes of Indians across the sub-continent. Their involvement with corporate social responsibility amounts to an expenditure of $ 30 million a year. By a rough estimate, the Tata Group as a whole, through its Companies and Trusts spends about 30 % of its Profits After Tax (PAT) on social upliftment schemes. According the PAT figures for 2003–04, the amount comes to Rs. 1700 crores. The principle involved is to give back to society what came from the people. There are several community initiatives undertaken by the various Tata companies. A few of these may be mentioned here viz., the anti-leprosy crusade in Jamshedpur, the handicraft development project in Okhamandal, Gujarat, helping

disabled children through their Tata Tea's organization Srishti, rehabili-
tation of maimed Indian soldiers of the Kargil war, earthquake victims of
Gujarat, supporting mentally ill homeless women in Chennai etc. There are
also various ecological projects undertaken by Tata companies in different
parts of the country.

The seed of industrial development was sown by Jamsetji Tata about
120 years back. Besides the industrial development, it has generated through
its various companies, it continues to provide succour to the distressed, disabled and marginalized sections in the far corners of India to this day. This
spiritual motivation and sensitivity to alleviate the pain and distress of others has not only been a passive emotion but has been translated into action
through several projects, thus transforming the lives of millions of people
over the last 100 years. His life reminds me of the words of Meister Eckhart
who had said "What we plant in the soil of contemplation, we shall reap
in the harvest of action".

2. Chapter

On Compassion: The Buddhist Approach

SAMDHONG RINPOCHE

To AVOID ANY CONFUSION because of the usage of language, I would like to clarify what exactly the word that the Buddhist use for 'Compassion'. The term 'Compassion' is western English group language expression which might have its own meaning, nuance if used as equivalence to the Sanskrit term '*Karuna*'. In Buddhism, we refer this unique state of mind or attitude which is called *Karuna* that may not be exactly the same meaning as the word 'compassion' with its traditional interpretation or connotation.

Karuna is that state of mental attitude which sees a problem or suffering of other sentient beings, and develops a strong wish to remove or to put an end to that suffering. Such mental attitude is termed as *Karuna*. *Karuna* can be categorized into three kinds according to the scope of goal or the objective, the intensity of the understanding of suffering and the intensity of the will to remove it.

a) *Karuna*

b) Immeasurable *Karuna* or *Aparmiya Karuna*, and then

c) *Maha-Karuna* or the Great *Karuna*.

So these are three different kind of compassion which the Buddhist follower tries to practice. As I mentioned that *Karuna* means a strong will to remove or put an end to suffering of someone else, the first requirement is the understanding of the nature of the suffering. The Buddha, after his enlightenment, spent seven weeks pondering upon how to communicate his *Nirvana* experience, the state of enlightenment, to a common man. After great deal of dialogue and consideration, he then decided to reveal his experience through setting the motion of the 'Wheel of Dharma' at Sarnath to his first five disciples. And the revelation or the sharing of his experience to his disciples was through the teaching of the *Caturāyasatya*, the Four Noble Truth. I am not sure whether the expression 'Noble' exactly communicates the meaning of *Arya* but I will use it for the sake of convenience.

The first truth is the truth of suffering. People do not understand the broader or the deeper part of the suffering. They only understand a very small portion of suffering. Therefore ordinary people like us do not have the will to put an end to our own suffering because we do not recognize our own suffering.

So the Budhha says the first truth, 'the truth of suffering', needs to be realized, and the second truth is 'the cause of suffering' which needs to be eradicated. The third, 'the truth of path' which need to be practiced, and finally the fourth truth, 'the truth of salvation', the truth of *moksha*, that is to be achieved.

So when Buddha said the truth of "*dukkha*", the suffering, needs to be understood, it means that the people do not understand the suffering. Our understanding of suffering is very superficial and inadequate. If you have read about Buddha's life story, it is quite clear that the young prince Siddhartha when he set out from the palace one day, he happens to see a very sick person, a dead body and old, aged person which he immediately related to himself and to the entire humanity. He has that sensitivity to understand these sufferings and almost instantly give up the luxuries of a kingdom to set out in search of the path through which all these miseries or these "*dukkhas*" could be put to an end, not only for him but for entire living beings. We see all these things almost every day but we do not relate them to ourselves and we do not realize that these are real sufferings. It becomes a kind of usual happening that need not be given serious consideration. The Suffering of Suffering, which in Sanskrit is called "*Dukh dukh*" that means the visible pain which we experience in the form of disease, decay, death, poverty & so many things, these visible pain which we have the capability of understanding it better, yet we still do not perceive or experience them deeply enough. It is because we seek temporary relief. When you suffer from great pain due to disease, you get medical treatment and after few days when you are cured, you tend to forget the pain and never to take care of putting that suffering altogether to an end and eliminate the cause of the disease.

The second kind of misery or the suffering is known as 'the Changing Misery' or '*Parinam Dukha*'. All the worldly pleasures comes under this category: the health condition, the wealth whatever it may be, are all impermanent and bound to decay and disintegrate, come to an end. A person may remain powerful all his lifetime, as an emperor or as a ruler or as rich person, but no one has the capacity or potential to avoid death. Death is certain even in the 21st century and it will remain certain and true for all the times to come. The living creatures will not be able to find a way to preserve this body forever. So whatever be the worldly pleasure is bound to decay and cease, come to an end and at that time the whole pleasure is gone and the intense pain as result of losing all these so called happiness & pleasure will come forth. So all worldly pleasures are considered to be a second kind of misery because they are impermanent and they cause sufferings in the end. Our body is one of the greatest possessions that we have. Whatever worldly pleasure we experience, are being experienced through this body. When we have to leave this body, and since because we have enormous attachment to it, this will cause much more pain to us. So we shall have to understand the nature of worldly pleasure which is indeed a pain. The changing misery, or the *parinam dukh*, is a greater *dukh* than "*dukh dukh*". "*Dukh Dukh*" might be avoided; if you are careful, you might remain free from diseases all the life. But you cannot avoid the death. The healthy and beautiful body that you cherish shall have to be given up in the end.

The third kind of misery is our lack of freedom. We cannot decide by ourselves when to be born, when to leave, how long we shall live, when we are going to die. All are being determined by the force of *karma* and the *klesas;* the mental defilements and resultant action will decide of the life. We do not have any freedom; nothing can go at our will. The karmic force is the result of the good deeds '*kushala karma*' and the bad deeds '*Akushala karma*' accumulated over a time because of our mental defilements, the *Klesas.* So we are completely under the bondage of Karma and *Klesas,* and have no freedom. That is the greatest misery for un-enlightened person, a bondage person. So this *Sanskara Dukh*, the misery of the pervasive bondage, the lack of freedom that is the basis of all other miseries and that bondage is represented or manifested in the form of our body. So our body is the basis of all our entire sufferings. It may be the suffering of disease or decay or accident or anxieties, or whatever it may be, all these things are dependent on our body and our association with body is not at our will, it is given by the Karmic force and it will cease by the Karmic force. When at the time of death you cannot ask few minutes more to wait because the karmic force will take you to the death. So this dependency and lack of freedom is the pervasive misery and all this misery shall have to be realized and experienced and we must have a wish or will to eradicate these miseries. Unless a person does not understand one's own misery, he or she cannot understand the other's misery.

But having said that karmic forces shape the courses of our lives, however our actions are not bound by the *Karma* and *Klesas*. Of course unless you have eradicated your *Kleshas*, your actions might be contaminated by the *Klesas*, yet you have the freedom to act in any way, in a positive way or in a negative way. So a portion of freedom is present in this life, but what I am talking about, absence of freedom is once your Karmic force has given the result, the *Karam vipak,* the fruition of *Karma.* When *Karam vipak* is already grown up or ripe, then you cannot alter it, for example, our mind's relation with our body, we cannot cease at our will but we can do something. We can practice the *marg* to put this bondage or this relation to an end. We cannot do it by our will but we can do *Sadhana*, the practice to put it to an end, so therefore we shall have to differentiate how much freedom is there and how much bondage is there, there are very clear distinctions between the two.

And in understanding the misery, understanding the *dukh-satya*, the truth of misery, is first step towards achieving a compassionate mind, *Karuna.* When you have desire to eradicate your own sufferings then you shall think about others as well, then the self and others are all equal on many grounds. Each sentient being are one and the same in not liking suffering and desiring happiness and pleasure; there is no difference between any human whether he is a king or laymen, or for that matter any living beings be it a small insect or the elephant. Everyone has this tendency to avoid misery and embrace pleasure & happiness. This is a universal truth and based on this there is no difference among all sentient beings.

How much you are suffering, the same agony is being suffered by all bonded person. There is no difference. If we remember that it is not just ourselves but everyone who has to undergo suffering, this more realistic perspective will increase our determination and capacity to overcome troubles. So therefore when you have a will to put to an end to your suffering, then you can cultivate a will to remove suffering of others as well on the basis of that equality. That is the first stage of compassionate mind or the *Karuna*. But if your *Karuna* may be towards only a few people, few individual living beings who may be your loved ones, then such kind of compassionate mind and a will to remove suffering of your relatives, perhaps your loved ones is just an ordinary small steps of compassion. When you enlarge this kind of feeling for immeasurable people or immeasurable livings beings, then your compassion becomes kind of immeasurable compassion because the object of compassion being immeasurable. However if you are not taking the entirety of sentient beings within the purview of your compassion, though it may be construed as immeasurable compassion, it is not the greatest or the *Maha-Karuna*.

Acharya Shantideva describes meditation on *Karuna* as thus: "Strive at first to meditate upon the sameness of yourself and others. In joy and sorrow all are equal; Thus be guardian of all, as of yourself. The hand and other limbs are many and distinct, but all are one – the body to kept and guarded. Likewise, different beings, in their joys and sorrows, are like me, all one in wanting happiness. This pain of mine does not afflict or cause discomfort to another's body, and yet this pain is hard for me to bear because I cling and take it for my own. And other beings' pain I do not feel, and yet, because I take them for myself, their suffering is mine and therefore hard to bear. And therefore I will dispel the pain of others, for it is simply pain, just like my own. And others I will aid and benefit, for they are living beings, like my body. Since I and other beings both, in wanting happiness, are equal and alike, what difference is there to distinguish us, that I should strive to have my bliss alone?"

So when you take the entirety of sentient beings within your purview of your will to remove the misery then that is called *Maha-Karuna* and which combines a little bit different attitude of not only wishing to remove the misery of entire world, entire sentient beings, but also taking the responsibility that I will do whatever it takes to remove the misery of entire essential beings. That is called *Maha-Karuna* and through which we achieve *Bodhichitta*. *Bodhichitta* means inspiration for achieving Buddha nature, because without achieving Buddha nature you cannot remove entire sentient beings misery. Only an enlightened Buddha can do that. So therefore the inspiration or the will to attain the Buddhahood or *Nirvana* is not an end in itself but as a means to serve the entire sentient beings. In

a nutshell, a strong determined will that seeks to remove the entire misery
– not only the apparent misery but the changing misery and the basis of
misery, this entirety which is bothering the whole sentient beings - and to
take this responsibility onto oneself to put to an end to all this miseries and
for which one practices the entirety of *Bodhisattvachariya*, the activities of
the *bodhisattva*, this kind of mind set or attitude is called *Maha-Karuna*.
The *Maha-Karuna*, the great compassion does not see any differentiation
between self and the others and it will also understand the interdependent-
ness of every living being. Even if you wish to remove your own misery,
you cannot remove your own misery without removing the misery of others. The miseries are all interdependent, the path are all interdependent,
even your need to achieve the Buddha-hood is only possible with the help
of the innumerable sentient beings. The entire living creatures are absolutely interdependent, they have very subtle or gross relationship with each
other and that relationship is the basis of great compassion and the mutation of *Karuna* to *Maha-Karuan*.

So once you achieve the mind set which is called the *Maha-Karuna*,
then there will be no division, there will be no discrimination, there will
be no near or far because the entire sentient beings shall have to be within
the purview of your *Karuna*, within your will to put an end to their misery
and I think that kind of mind set is the basis for not only human solidarity,
it will be basis for solidarity of entire sentient beings. His Holiness the
Dalai Lama says "True compassion is not just an emotional response but
a firm commitment founded on reason. Therefore, a truly compassionate
attitude towards others does not change even if other behaves negatively."

The question arises that if compassion is good and it is pertinent in
all religion, then why it is not being practiced? I think it is not just about
compassion. All the religious values or teachings are not being practiced
by its so-called followers. It is my assumption that religions have already
disappeared from the face of earth, what remains is just the names and the
institutions of religion. Therefore the names of religious have become the
source of division. Actually religion is a very loose term; it encompasses
all the three things, the religiousness, religionosity & the religionism, or
the creed, code, cult community. All three things are being mixed up and
combined in the name of religion. So the religiousness has disappeared. I
can't talk for other religious traditions but I can only say that Buddhism,
I think there are very, very few Buddhist people on this earth today. The

Buddha dharma has already disappeared, what we have now is huge Buddha statues, enormous monasteries and buildings and temples and people wearing robes, apart from the real *aagama* – the teaching in words – and *aadhigama* – the practice in the mind. These two things are absolutely missing today. If the religions are there and if the people become really religious, then there cannot be any division; Division is absolutely impossible.

The concept and dynamics of compassion need not necessarily have to be understood solely through religion. The teaching of compassionate mind without putting it within the different religious parameter, I think that can be done as His Holiness the Dalai Lama has been working and advocating secular ethics or secular good-mind. To become more compassionate towards others, His Holiness says "we do not need to become religious, nor do we need to believe in an ideology. All that is necessary is for each of us to develop our good human qualities." The compassionate mind need not necessarily combined with any religious frame work. Any secular, even a non-believer, can have a loving and cared mind for others because without which no one can survive. This is a secular fact that we as newly born, if our mother did not care of us, if she does not have a loving kindness for us, we could not have survived. We couldn't have become a matured person. And similarly we are dependent entirely on the other beings for our identity, for our survival, for our happiness. To highlight our interdependences, His Holiness reasons "even the smallest insects are social beings who without any religion, law or education, survive by mutual cooperation based on an innate recognition of their interconnectedness. All phenomena from the planet we inhabit to the oceans, clouds, forests and flowers that surround us, arise in dependence upon subtle pattern of energy. Without their proper interaction, they dissolve and decay." "Ultimately the reason why love and compassion bring the greatest happiness is simply that our nature cherishes them above all else. The need for love lies at the very foundation of human existence." So there is no need of religious belief, any rational person can understand that without care and compassionate mind, no one can survive.

In practice of Compassion, tolerance is one important aspect. But in the world, there has always been a one set of people who go on creating disturbance and violence. How should we deal with them? Tolerance, in Buddhist concept, has no limitation. We call it *Kshanti Paramita – paramita* meaning limitless. So for example those who may be breaking the statue of Buddha and whatever they may do, the perpetrator, the person has to be tolerated and needs to be seen as object of tolerance, not only tolerance, but object of compassion, however his actions to be opposed. As mentioned earlier, the action of breaking Buddha's statue need to be condemned or needs to be stopped, if possible. Otherwise it at least should be disapproved of. But one thing, breaking of Buddha's statue does not harm the Buddha dharma. Buddha dharma is inside the minds of the people and nobody can take it away. The monasteries may be burnt, the statues maybe smashed and the monks may be killed, but the killing of the monk does not mean killing the Buddhism. The monk will carry Buddhism in his mind and in his continuity of *chitta* and it will remain.

As a Buddhist, not accepting injustice is a part of our Dharma. If somebody is doing injustice and you are not opposing to that act of injustice, then you are also a silent approver of that injustice which means you become a party to that injustice. Wherever injustice is done, a Buddhist or a religious minded person shall have to express his/her disapproval and opposition to it. That is the religious duty. But for that it must be combined by a compassionate mind toward that actor. We should only condemn the action, not the actor. The actor is a subject of compassion and the action is to be opposed. It is very essential to make this distinction. A Buddhist monk roaming in the street with full of anger, is not an engaged Buddhist. It is totally disengaged from Buddhist values to show anger to the actors, the injustice doers. This is not Buddhism.

Buddhism has no special or particular mechanism to oppose or fight the injustice. Our mechanism is quite similar to the mechanism that Mahatma Gandhi has adopted. To condemn injustice or immoral act, there are few different ways to condemn that action and dissociate oneself from the actors and action both, not speaking with the injustice doers, not using the food and shelter together with them and making speeches with reasons how these actions are bad. These are non-violently way to dissociate oneself, so these methods can vary from time to time and from social system to social system.

Discrimination of any kind is a potential element that breeds hatred and violence. Buddha has addressed strongly against the discrimination between caste, race, creed or classes and he promoted the equality of every sentient being on the basis of its potential and as I mentioned before, he also talked about the equality on the basis of our wants and don't wants. Therefore discriminating anyone is the violence and is against the Buddha dharma. His Holiness often teaches that "Right to overcome suffering and to be happy is equal to one's own. When you recognize that all beings are equal in both their desire for happiness and their right to obtain it, you automatically feel empathy and closeness for them. As long as they are human beings experiencing pleasure and pain just as you do, there is no logical basis to discriminate between them or to alter your concern for them if they behave negatively." So non-discrimination and treat everyone equally is the basis of the Buddha dharma. That is the basis of non-violence as well. Therefore, Buddhism cannot approve any kind of competition. Competition is the worst kind of violence. Compare and compete, this is curse of modern civilization which Mahatma Gandhi has very clearly said Modern civilization is the *Kalyuga* civilization according to Hindu view. And it is *shaitanik* civilization according to Muslims. So the civilization which is built on competition and comparison – competition means get oneself to win and other to lose – is not compatible and it is not allowed in the Buddhism in any way.

In conclusion, I want to recall here the teachings of His Holiness the Dalai Lama who explains in very simple term why we need to have compassionate mind and how it is beneficial to oneself. He says the purpose of our life is to be happy. From the very core of our being, we simply desire contentment. Therefore, it is important to discover what will bring about the greatest degree of happiness. Every kind of happiness and suffering can be divided into two main categories of mental and physical. It is the mind that exerts the greatest influence on us so we should devote our most serious efforts to bringing about mental peace. The more we care for the happiness of others, the greater our own sense of well-being becomes. Cultivating a close, warm-hearted feeling for others automatically puts the mind at ease. This helps remove whatever fears or insecurities we may have and gives us the strength to cope with any obstacles we encounter. It is the ultimate source of success in life.

3. Chapter

Compassion – A Complement to Wisdom

IN THIS SHORT PRESENTATION I will try to present a clear picture of the concept of compassion, which is really like the heart of Buddhist practice. It is my humble expectation that such sharing of knowledge will not only contribute towards enriching our theoretical ideas and gathering information but will help minimise human miseries much of which is unfortunately man made and therefore unwanted. I would therefore first of all like to thank the organisers, hosts and the learned participants.

I. Compassion is the root of Mahayana path

The highest goal for a Buddhist practitioner is to actualise Buddhahood. It is not possible for omniscience to be produced without causes, because if it were everything could always be omniscient. If things were produced without reliance on something else, they could exist without constraint – there would be no reason why everything could not be omniscient. Therefore, since all functional things arise only occasionally, they depend strictly on their causes. Omniscience too is rare because it does not occur at all times and in all places, and everything cannot become omniscient. Therefore, it definitely depends on causes and conditions.

Also from among these causes and conditions, you should cultivate correct and complete causes. If you put the wrong causes into practice, even if you work hard for a long time, the desired goal cannot be achieved. It will be like milking a (cow's) horn. Likewise, the result will not be produced when all the causes are not put into effect. For example, if the seed or any other cause is missing, then the result, a sprout, and so forth, will not be produced. Therefore, those who desire a particular result should cultivate its complete and unmistaken causes and conditions.

If you ask, 'What are the causes and conditions of the final fruit of omniscience?' I, who am like a blind man, may not be in a position to explain (by myself), but I shall employ the Buddha's own words just as he spoke them to his disciples after his enlightenment. He said, „Vajrapani, Lord of Secrets, The transcendental wisdom of omniscience has its root in compassion, arises from a cause – the altruistic thought, the awakening mind of bodhichitta and the perfection of skillful means." Therefore, if you are interested in achieving omniscience, you need to practice these three: compassion, the awakening mind of bodhichitta and skillful means. Moved by compassion, Bodhisattvas take the vow to liberate all sentient beings.

Then by overcoming their self-centered outlook, they engage eagerly and continuously in the very difficult practices of accumulating merits and insights.

Having entered into this practice they will certainly complete the collection of merit and insight. Accomplishing the accumulation of merit and insight is like having omniscience itself in the palm of your hand. Therefore, since compassion is the only root of omniscience, you should become familiar with this practice from the very beginning.

The *Compendium of Perfect Dharma* reads, "O Buddha, a Bodhisattva should not train in many practices. If a Bodhisattva properly holds to one Dharma and learns it perfectly, he has all the Buddha's qualities in the palm of his hand. And, if you ask what that one Dharma is, it is great compassion."

The Buddhas have already achieved all their own objectives, but remain in the cycle of existence for as long as there are sentient beings. This is because they possess great compassion. They also do not enter the immensely blissful abode of nirvana like the Hearers. Considering the interests of sentient beings first, they abandon the peaceful abode of nirvana as if it were a burning iron house. Therefore, great compassion alone is the unavoidable cause of the non-abiding Nirvana of the Buddha.

Compassion is important in the beginning, middle and in the end as is stated in the following verse in *Entering the Middle way by Chandrakirti:*

"Before all else I praise compassion;
for this alone is the seed of the excellent harvest (which is) the conquerors,

as the water that nourishes (this crop),
and as the ripened fruit that is ready for use."

II. The importance of compassion in the beginning

Once your mind is moved by great compassion, you will definitely make
the commitment to free all living beings from cyclic existence. If your compassion is weak, you will not. Therefore, compassion is important in the
beginning because feeling responsible to free all beings requires great compassion and because, if you do not take on this responsibility, you are not
ranked as a Mahayana practitioner. In this vein, the *Teachings of Aksaya-
mati Sutra (Aksayamatinirdesa-sutra)* states:

> "Furthermore, Venerable sariputra, the great compassion of the bodhisattvas is in-
> exhaustible. Why? Because it is the prerequisite.
> Venereable Shariputra, just as the movement of the breath is the prerequisite for life
> force of a human being, the great compassion of the bodhisattvas is the prerequisite
> for correctly reaching the Mahayana.

III. The importance of compassion in the middle

You may develop the spirit of enlightenment at one time and then engage
in the bodhisattva deeds. But when you see that living beings are innumerable and act improperly, that the training is very difficult and limitless,
and that you need an immeasurable length of time, you may lose heart and
fall into a lower path. However, by accustoming yourself to increasingly
greater compassion that is not just a one-time development, you become
less concerned with your own hapopiness or suffering and are not discour-
aged at providing other's welfare. Therefore you easily accomplish all the
collections.

IV. The importance of compassion at the end

Based on the power of great compassion, buddhas, even when they reach
their goal, do not abide in peace just for oneself but continue to work for
the welfare of beings as long as space remains. For without compassion
buddhas would be like sravakas, Kamalashila's second Stages of Meditation says:

With this powerful idea in view, the Compendium of the Teachings Sutra (Dharma-samgiti-sutra) says: "Bhagavan, bodhisattavs shout not."

Thus compassion is the basis of engaging in the deeds because when you see that you will not live up to your commitment without training in the two vast collections, of merit and wisdom, you set about the difficult work of amassing these vast collections. The principal cause of the aspirational Bodhichitta are compassion and love, which are essentially the desire that you and all other beings be free from misery and have happiness (and are instigated by the miseries of samsara), as indicated in the Crown of Great Vehicle Sutras: "The rivers of compassion and love truly spring from misery itself."

V. The process of mind training in the stages of the path of great individual (Mahayana)

Atisha's Lamp of the Path (Bodhipathpradipa) states:

> Through the realization of the sufferings within oneself
> One who wishes to thoroughly put an end to
> All the sufferings of others
> Such a person is a supreme individual.

In the stage by stage practice of the path three types of practitioners have been identified. In the case of the middle individual, out of fear towards the suffering of samsara a genuine wish to get liberated from it is developed and by training their mind only by the path of the middle individual such a person seeks peace (nirvana) only for oneself. However in the training of the mind in the path of a great individual by inferring from the suffering within oneself one is unable to tolerate the fact that others are also suffering in the same way as oneself. One then aspires that they be freed from suffering and undertake one's practices accordingly. Such a person is referred to as a great individual (Mahapurusha). The Concise Wisdom Perfection Sutra states:

> The two paths which do not have the capacity to fulfill the purposes of the world
> Should be forever abandoned
> The compassionate path taught by the Victor is thus entered by
> Those who are in the nature of one pointed concentration to benefit others.

As stated in this sutra, by practicing the path of adopting and abandoning the four truths liberation is achieved. However by that even one's own purpose is not completed as such the extensive purpose of benefitting others is not possible. Hence without entering the path of the sravakas and pratyeka buddhas which do not have the capacity to accomplish far reaching purposes of others one should enter the Mahayana and accomplish the purposes of others as is taught in the *Epistle to the Student by the Tibetan teacher Ridawa:*

> Even the animals eat for themselves few morsels of grass that are extremely rare to find
> Even those tormented by great thirst when found water enjoys it with delight and satisfaction
> The greatness of an individual is found in the case of those who endeavour to fulfill other's purposes
> Such an individual will be in peace and such skill of an individual makes one excel from others.
> Like the supremely beneficial sun which moves in the space and gives light
> And like the earth that lifts the world without seeing it as a burden
> The nature of great beings without selfishness is like that
> They one pointedly enter into bringing the well being and benefiting the world.

As said above fulfilling the well-being of just this life is found even among animals. Hence the potential and skill of great individuals should be like the sun and the moon that dispels the darkness and the great earth that lifts the world. Thus with great courage one takes the responsibility of others and there what is inevitable is stated in the *Living the Bodhisattva Way of Life*:

> When Bodhicitta is developed, then instantaneously
> Those who are helpless and bound in the prison of cyclic existence
> Will be addressed as the child of those Gone into Peace (Tathagata)
> And becomes object of homage by god and man of the world.

Thus it is taught that even someone wandering in samsara with suffering becomes a Bodhisattva immediately on developing the mind. In the absence of Bodhicitta whatever other qualities like the precious superior trainings one may have, one does not get enlisted among the category of Mahayana. This is as is taught in *Maitreya's Uttaratantra* (Sublime Continuum):

> The appreciation in the supreme vehicle as the seed and wisdom
> Is like the mother producing the Buddha's qualities and those that

Abide in the calm womb of concentration and with the mother of compassion
Whoever possess these are the children born from the Buddha.

Water and manure are common cause for producing various grains and
a mother who is of particular lineage gives birth to various children of
different castes. The uncommon cause like the seed grain and a Brahmin
father should be of definite lineage. Just as there cannot be wheat sprout by
planting barley or a child of different caste from a Brahmin father likewise
in order to get liberated from cyclic existence through any of the Hinayana
or Mahayana, wisdom realizing selflessness and so forth are needed in both
and are therefore like the mother. However this Bodhicitta, which is like
the father, the uncommon cause of the Buddha is similar to a precious vajra
that dispels all the downfalls of samsara and nirvana and hence excels all
other ordinary ornaments. In order to practise this stages of the path of
the great individual there are two processes: The process of how to develop
the mind to enlightenment and the process of training in the conduct after
having developed the mind. The process of how to develop the mind to
enlightenment has two: Stages of Training in the mind to enlightenment
and the process of holding the mind development through ritual.

VI. Stages of Training in the mind to enlightenment

In general the factor for generation of the mind is directly seeing the qualities of the Buddha and Bodhisattavas. Having heard the Bodhisattava
pitakas even if one has not directly seen them, even if one has not heard
them in greater details nut having heard roughly the reasons of inevitabil-
ity of this teaching for achieving Buddhahood and thus unable to tolerate
the disappearance of the Mahayana teaching. Even if the process of decli-
nation of the teaching may not have started, however in this extremely bad
time of degeneration it is even difficult to find the generation of mind to
enlightenment of the sravakas and pratyeka-buddhas. Hence what need to
talk about the unsurpassing enlightenment. Thinking thus the mind wishing to attain Buddhahood is generated. Mind generation is done in reliance
to the four causes of lineage, spiritual teacher, compassionate heart and
absence of discouragement. Through one's power, through the power of
others, the causal power of habituation in Mahayana in the past lives,
the power of application of habituation in virtuous deeds and thus many
causes and factors like the four causes and four powers have been taught.

Now a days the main practice relies on the two, the seven cause effect instruction transmitted from the great Jowo and the instruction passed through Bodhisattava Shantideva. The reason for training the mind in the seven cause effect instruction of the great Jowo's system is thus: the state of Buddhahood comes from the mind of enlightenment and that comes from special attitude, that comes from compassion, that comes from loving kindness, that comes from repaying the kindness, that comes from remembering the kindness, that comes from recognizing as the mother. Thus such an order has an essential meaning. However there is no definiteness that the great compassion would arise only in between special attitude and loving kindness and not otherwise as is stated in Entering the Middle Way:

> Because for this perfect crop of the Victorious, compassion alone
> Is accepted like the seed, the water for the development
> And the fruit for continuous and prolonged enjoyment
> As such I praise the compassion first.

Thus it is not only making commitment in the beginning to liberate sentient beings from the samsara which is dependent on compassion but in between not to get astrayed into lower path due to discouragement due to difficulty of the deed and finally even after enlightenment, not remaining in peace like the sravakas and the pratyeka Buddhas and absence of discouragement in accomplishing the purposes of all sentient beings is also dependent upon great compassion.

Moreover in order to develop compassion in this way there should be a feeling of dearness in the heart by which all sentient beings are recognized as mother. Even individuals who had not trained in these paths develop superficial love and compassion by reflecting and remembering the kindness of relatives like one's mother. However not only it is not developed towards enemies and so forth with which one is in disharmony but contrarily even develops a wish that they encounter suffering and be without happiness.

Hence in our case also if we do not cultivate equanimity in the beginning even if we pretend to be meditating on the path, loving kindness and compassion will become partial. Therefore as an antidote to this first of all meditate on equanimity.

One might here think and even ask that if loving-kindness is to be cultivated towards the mother and so forth then what use is there to stop the loving mind that we have now. In the case of the loving kindness within the seven cause-effect, it should not be mixed with attachment even to the slightest degree. The love that we have right now in our mind is motivated by attachment. For example in an uneven ground you cannot live properly or your stay will not be comfortable likewise to someone whose mind is uneven due to attachment and hatred there will be no opportunity to have loving kindness. Moreover here we are not talking about meditating on equanimity of feeling and so on but on immeasurable equanimity where one's mind is free from attachment and hatreds towards sentient beings first of all visualize well a sentient being who is neither friend nor enemy. When his facial shape and manner and so forth arises in the mind then focusing on when the thought of hatred and love is allowed to develop Both the hatred that sees it as unpleasant and the attachment that sees it as pleasant will not be very powerful. If there is slight difference in degree of the two, apply antidote for whichever is greater and meditate until the mind becomes even. Thus in the beginning meditate towards the neutral and this is done from the point of easier cultivation as to that object there is greater equanimity. Then use a sworn enemy and a very close friend as the object of focus and then when a manifest thought of attachment and hatred arises towards them, reflect well how the enemies also acted as friends in the past lives and benefited you many times and how the friends also have become your enemies in the past lives and harmed you by killing and so forth and through this way the thought of attachment and hatred are equalized. However if one has developed experience regarding the uncertainty of enemy and friend during the practice of the middle individual it seems here it will be very easy to sustain the visualization. Just like driving away one hundred birds with one slang if an effortlessly equalizing mind is developed towards all sentient beings just with these three objects then it is enough. Still if you find it difficult to develop it is crucial to meditate by moving on different types. In this way having equalized total hatred and attachment towards all sentient beings who are enemies, relatives and neutral, first of all to prepare the basis of the mind aspiring to fulfill the purposes of others and in order to know all sentient beings as mother reflect in this way. Just as there is no end to cycle of existence there is no end to my lives. Hence when you reflect that there is no life which I have not taken after having conceived in the womb of all sentient beings it will arise due to the power of imagination. However since it is difficult to develop conviction by meditating in general, visualize your present mother itself in front as she is: old, young, shape, costumes and manner. Just as it is evident that this one has acted as your mother of this life likewise she has done so in many other lives as well. For example, in the sutra it is stated how the mother of Tathagata's present life has acted as mother many life times during the path of training. Thinking that the words of a valid individual are non-deceiving and if one meditates through inference, an indepth and special conviction will be developed. Then by meditating also on other types of sentient beings like the father, relatives, neutral ones, enemies and hell-beings then finally an uncontrived mind that recognizes all sentient beings as mother and which perceives them similar like the mother of this life will arise.

Having developed experience in this, recollect kindness. This mother has carried me in her womb for ten months duration, sacrificed her well-being, hunger, thirst and so forth. All her beneficial and harmful actions were done for the sake of the child and has given this very body and life with leisure and freedom and thus she is greatly kind in the beginning of the child's life. Having born from the womb she places the child on soft cloth bedding, sustained by loving mind, gazes with loving eye, welcomes with joyous smile, call by sweet name, feeds with sweet breast milk, foods are fed by tongue, mucus are cleaned by mouth, filths are wiped by hand, caresses to the warmth of the flesh and protects from the fear of fire, water and cliff. She wholeheartedly prefers her illness than her child and her death than her child. She looks after you in this way and thus is greatly kind in between. After grown up she takes care of the child's education concerning manner of eating, manner of going and so forth are taught by herself or requests others to teach. She offers everything like land, house, wealth and property that are dear like the heart to her and which she sought with much effort until her flesh gets strained and after enduring sins, sufferings and bad reputations and thus greatly kind at the end. Reflecting on these, meditate until tears fall from eyes, hairs of the body stand on end and your mind becomes fully concerned. Then reflect gradually from one's father to enemy and towards all sentient beings of the six kinds and how they have acted, as is done in this way by the present mother, when they have acted as mother countless times. Although all these that has been just mentioned are not there in the case of animals and so on, it seems the intention is from the point view that there is no one who has not acted as mother each time when they were born as a human being.

Having developed experience in remembering the kindness, repay the kindness as is stated in the *Epistle to the Student:*

> While seeing the relatives entrapped within the ocean of suffering
> Like fallen deep into the ocean
> If you leave them for not recognizing due to change of life
> And attempt only for personal freedom, there will be nothing more embarrassing and shameful than this.

As stated the mind of the mother sentient beings are disturbed by the evil spirit of afflictive emotions, their eye of discrimination is blinded by ignorance. They are without the rhythm of the profound and sublime dharma. They are left by the guide of spiritual masters who guide them to the city of liberation, and they have slipped from the place of higher rebirth and liberation and fallen into the abyss of cyclic existence. These beings that are wandering in the prison of three sufferings, except that we do not recognize them due to change of life, they are all our kind mothers who had benefited us in many lives. If these mothers do not put their hope in me to whom should they put their hope? If the responsibility of taking care of these mothers does not fall on me to whom else will it fall? For example, if one's parents, or close friends of this life gets entrapped in prison, or in an isolated place where there is danger of robbers, thieves or wild animals and while you have the means to free them, if you mentally abandon them and remain relaxed, there will be nothing more lacking in shame and embarassment than this as is stated in the *Verses of Drum Sound of King of Naga:*

> Oceans, mount meru
> And the earths are not my burden
> Not repaying the kindness
> Is my great burden.

Hence think that while I have the capacity to protect the kind mothers if I leave them and enter a lower path, which aspires peace for oneself alone, the mind of the great beings will be embarrassed from the depth. Therefore I will give that up and practise the ways to benefit towards all sentient beings. If you ask, how to benefit? By dispelling the suffering under different situations like giving food for the hungry, drink for the thirsty, medicine for the sick and wealth and goods for those who are deprived of it. These are causes for one's own collection of merit and hence it is not that you should not do them. But if you regard making sentient beings meet with the worldly power and wealth as the main way of benefiting them,it is wrong. They have been Brahma, and the biggest evil force, Garab Wangchuk, of the desire realm and even a universal monarch countless times. Howevere by having not achieved stability they are under such a situation of suffering of poverty, heat and cold. If I also put them primarily to contaminated happiness, the greater their power and wealth there will be greater risk of the happiness changing into suffering. It will be similar like putting a hot substance into a wound by which the suffering increases. Therefore think that I will put them either to the state of liberation or omniscience and contemplate until you develop definite mental changes. It is not enough to simply prepare the ground/basis in this way for the development of the mind aspiring to benefit others. In order to develop the actual mind you need the three, loving kindness, compassion and special attitude. In the case of the two, loving kindness and compassion it is related to any mind which arises wishing to put sentient beings to happiness and wishing to separate them from suffering. There is no definite cause effect sequence. However in general practice loving kindness is treated first. *Precious Garland by Nagarjuna* states:

> Even the three times a day giving of
> Foods of three hundred pots
> In no way can match the merits
> Of a short moment's loving-kindness.
> Gods and man will love
> The will also guard you
> There will be mental peace and much happiness
> Free from the harms of poisons and weapons
> One's purposes will be achieved without effort
> And will be born in the Braham world
> Even if not liberated
> The eight qualities of love will be achieved.

Thus meditating on love, which has infinite benefits is to reflect how the mother of this life is without happiness. Irrespective of whether she has obvious sufferings like illness, poverty or not she is one with suffering of change and conditioned suffering. Develop an intense mind wishing this mother who is without happiness, to put to happiness and verbally say 'How nice if these elderly mothers meet with happiness. May they meet with happiness. By any means I will make them meet with happiness'. Repeat this many times and contemplate in this way. Similarly one should meditate towards sentient beings, without distinction, like enemy and friends in accordance with the previous teachings. Things like presence and absence of manifest sufferings in the three bad migrations and suffering and suffering in the happy migration should be referred in accordance with the situation. However if you think that since the enemy has harmed me in such and such way he is not worth of benefiting then it is important to think whether this is a retribution of the harms that I have done in my past lives or is it due to the provocation of his mind by the afflictive emotions and thus total lack of freedom with himself. If the mother or a relative of this life hurls weapon and so forth to you due to madness of evil spirit, then to that not only not becoming angry one will attempt the means to get rid of the evil spirit. Likewise reflect that this old mother of the past lives, which is imputed as enemy in the mistaken perspective of this (worldly) appearance, is also maddened by the evil force of afflictive emotions. How nice if she meets with happiness by getting rid of this evil force and practise as before is the main point. If you question and doubt thinking that since earlier even the enemies have been already meditated as mother, it will not be difficult to develop loving kindness. This is total lack of examination. It is evident that some shameless people kill even their mother of this life and see her as enemy and do many harms.

Having meditated on compassion towards all sentient beings, compassion focuses on the mother of this life who is tormented by any of the three sufferings. Alas! my mother of this life is directly harmed by suffering and indirectly harmed by its origin and thus does not have even the slightest opportunity of happiness. Thinking how nice if she is freed from this suffering verbally say 'How nice if all these old mother sentient beings afflicted by suffering are freed from suffering. May they be free from suffering. By any means I will help them get rid of suffering.' In this way repeat many times and mentally contemplate. Contemplate by switching towards all, enemies and friends. *The Great Stages of the Path by Tsong Khapa* states that if one has gained confidence of the practices of small and middle individual then by inferring through one's own experiences all these practices will become easier to meditate. The mere wish that sentient beings meet with happiness and be free from suffering is there even in the ordinary beings. Only this is not enough as such the two practices, loving kindness and compassion are needed as just mentioned. It is a loving kindness and compassion that has the capacity to bring forth genuine special attitude that thinks 'I will practise thus'.

The genuine special attitude brought forth by these two is not just a mind wishing to free sentient beings from suffering and put them in the state of happiness but it is a form of a commitment thinking I will myself do it without fail. Thinking, Alas, I will bear the responsibility of making these loving sentient beings meet with happiness and free from suffering and verbally say 'These mother sentient beings who are without happiness I will make them meet with happiness. These sentient beings who are afflicted by suffering I will make them free from suffering'. Due to the power of many repetitions and generation of pure attitude with mental commitment and by recalling the qualities of body, speech, mind and sublime activity as explained during taking refuge, when aspirational mind to supreme enlightenment is generated by thinking 'if I attain this state possessing this special qualities I will also be possible to liberate sentient beings'. It is similar to the mind generation which starts the practice for the three countless aeons. If you think since during the repaying of kindness also there is the desire to put sentient beings to liberation, there is nothing special in special attitude. Just as the thinking that I will buy this article and actually buying it are not same. Likewise there is a difference between repaying the kindness and special attitude and thus such distinction must be made. In this way if the mind is well trained through the seven cause effect practice then except in the process of explanation, Shantideva's system is also present here in terms of the meaning. So there is no definite need to have them separately. However since in the Great and Small Stages of the Path both the systems are taught and since they are practiced due to varied mental dispositions of the followers, the exchange of oneself to others in reliance upon the texts of the Bodhisattava Shantideva is as stated in Engaging the Bodhisattava Way of Life:

> One who wishes to quickly protect
> Oneself and others
> Practise the sublime secret
> Of exchanging oneself for others.
> All the happiness in the world
> They all arose from the wish that others be happy
> All the sufferings in the world
> They all resulted from the wish that I be happy.
> There is no need to elaborate

See the difference between these two:
The child who acts for himself
And the Conqueror, who acts for others.
If one's happiness and other's suffering
Are not genuinely exchanged
Not only Buddhahood itself is not actualized
But even in samsara there will be no peace.

Thus self-cherishing is the basis of all downfalls and cherishing others is the basis of all benefit and happiness and hence it is extremely important to practice. By judging the present state of not being able to bear even the minor reactions of other people to oneself, do not think that the mind of mere exchange of oneself to others will not arise:

Do not turn from difficulties
As when habituated in this way
Even the one who frightens you by just hearing his name
Will become one whose absence you will feel unhappy.

Take the example of an enemy with whom you are not in good terms and who merely by seeing makes you frightened and uncomfortable. But later when you come into good terms with him, your earlier attitude of disliking changes and he becomes an extremely pleasant person. Likewise through familiarity it is also possible to exchange oneself for the others. With regard to its practice, the meaning of exchanging oneself for others is like this. This practice does not mean to say that someone like Devadatta from his side should think that I am Dharmasvamin. But it is developing cherishing attitude to Dharmasvamin instead of the self-cherishing attitude to oneself, Devadatta, and to develop a mind that ignores it instead of ignoring Dharmasvamin. To this practice the name exchanging oneself for others is designated. Thus for the actual cycle of visualization, reflect that in the past until now, through the self-cherishing attitude, one's own purposes have been pursued and it had become a cause just for suffering and thus the attitude you developed on others should be applied to yourself and practice it. And the mind cherishing oneself should be transferred to others and practice it. It is taught that through habituation it will be possible to change the place of these two cherishing minds. For the sake of easier visualization practise as is taught in the Seven Points on Mind Training. *Nagarjuna's Precious Garland* similarly states:

May their misdeeds ripen on me
And may all my virtues ripen on them.

As is stated it seems the two, giving and receiving, were the main practices. So visualize the mother in front of oneself as earlier and then develop intense compassion focusing towards it. While breathing out from the right nostril imagine that all your contaminated virtues and happiness mounting on the horse of breath simultaneously enters through the left nostril of the mother in front and pervades throughout her body and mind and she obtains special peace. Again when you inhale from the left nostril, imagine that at the same time all the misdeeds, obscurations and sufferings are brought in through inhalation and arises within the heart as black heaps and the mother then possesses happiness without sufferings. In this way, train in it repeatedly in an inter-mixed form. Then practice specifically towards father, relatives, the neutral and enemies of this life and thus gradually all sentient beings of the six types. It is taught that right now we do not have much mental capacity but due to habituation a time will come when you will have no fear of giving everything, from food, clothing and house to even one's head, legs, hands and so on.

> Even the enemy, who pricks your heart like a thorn
> With the noble mind of equalising and exchanging oneself for the others
> One realizes how they are our beloved and close relatives and friends
> And thus the basis of biased and erroneous mind is annihilated.
> By giving up the mind that cherishes oneself
> And with the key of repaying benefit with harms
> The door of benefit and peace that spontaneously fulfills the two purposes
> Is simultaneously opened and this indeed is fortunate and amazing.

VII. Compassion and Attachment

The real or unique Compassion or sense of caring is unbiased and that mental attitude of closeness feeling develops not on the bases of whether some one is close to me or good for me or not. But rather with the recognition that the other one is also just like myself who wants happiness and do not want suffering or pain and also have the same right to overcome that suffering. On that recognition or awareness if we develop a sense of caring or a sense of concern that is the meaning of genuine compassion. So it is unbiased and here there is no hindrance of attachment. In our usual sense of love, compassion and closeness feeling there is much involvement of attachment. When attachment is involved, firstly it is biased and therefore it is very much dependent on other's attitude. When other's attitude is nice towards me then there comes attachment, if other's attitude is not so positive towards me then comes hatred. Tsongkhapa explains attachment like a drop of oil that falls on a piece of cloth. Once you develop attachment then it is very difficult to separate it from the object. You kind of get stuck there. How then one can have freedom. But as far as sense of caring or genuine compassion is concerned it is developed on the understanding that others are like you wanting happiness and not wanting suffering. So with that realisation irrespective of whatever is their attitude towards me but they also have the right to be happy. So there is a big difference between attachment and compassion. Attachment is not only biased but also very much due to mental projection. In reality the object may not be that nice but through your own mental projection it appears very nice and then you develop attachment. Compassion is developed on the basis of the understanding that although sentient beings are suffering, impermanent and devoid of an inherently existent self but they are unable to perceive this reality and thus suffer.

VIII. Secret of qualities like compassion

Familiarization and transformation of our behavior or our mind or first being aware of the value of positive transformation is important. Then second through awareness some kind of involvement in that value with conviction is crucial. If you get familiarized you will get used to it. Then without much difficulty we can implement. So first there should be awareness or knowledge and then through familiarization or as time goes one can get involved with that practice. Then that also is not sufficient still we need time to get used to it. That is the way to proceed forward in your practice. Of course when we start it is like learning ABCD and it is not at all easy but then eventually you don't find any difficulties. But it is after many months weeks and years of sustained practice that would bring some result. So similarly for actual transformation of any aspect of our behavior or mind all these factors like knowledge or awareness, and repeated practice and familiarization is needed. Eventually we can develop these qualities like compassion and wisdom.

IX. Meditation on Compassion

Meditative Stabilisation of Collecting all Merits Sutra states: That which liberates all sentient beings from all sufferings is great compassion. *Ratna Kutika Sutra* states: Great compassion is applied equally to all as it arose from a special sense of responsibility. Great compassion will engage honestly and without superficiality because it arose from the path. Great compassion will engage without crookedness as it arose from a stable mind without crookedness. It is thus: great compassion will engage in a way where it will relinquish personal wellbeing as it arose thoroughly from a sense of humility and respect to all sentient beings. Furthermore it states: great compassion will engage in the manner of taking the responsibility of all beings as it arose from a proper stability of enthusiastic effort. *Kamalashila's Stages of Meditation states:*

> The way to meditate on compassion will be taught from the outset. Begin the practice by meditating on equanimity. Try to actualize impartiality towards all sentient beings by eliminating attachment and hatred.
>
> All sentient beings desire happiness and do not desire misery. Think deeply about how, in this beginningless cycle of existence, there is not one sentient being who has not been my friend and relative hundreds of times. Therefore, since there is no ground for being attached to some and hating others, I shall develop a mind of equanimity towards all sentient beings.
>
> Begin the meditation on equanimity by thinking of a neutral person and then consider people who are friends and foes.
>
> After the mind has developed equanimity towards all sentient beings meditate on loving-kindness. Moisten the mental continuum with the water of loving-kindness and prepare it as you would a piece of fertile ground. When the seed of compassion is planted in such a mind, germination will be swift, proper and complete. Once you have irrigated the mind stream with loving-kindness, meditate on compassion.
>
> The compassionate mind has the nature of wishing all suffering beings to be free from suffering. Meditate on compassion for all sentient beings, because the beings in the three realms of existence are intensely tortured by the three types of sufferings in various forms. The Buddha has said that heat and other types of pain constantly torture beings in the hells for a very long time. He has also said that hungry ghosts are scorched by hunger and thirst and experience immense physical suffering. We can also see animals suffering in many miserable ways: they eat each other, become angry, and are hurt and killed. We can see that human beings too experience various acute kinds of pain. Not able to find what they want, they are resentful and harm each other. They suffer the pain of losing the beautiful things they want and confronting the ugly things they do not want, as well as the pain of poverty.

There are those whose minds are bound by various fetters of disturbing emotions like craving desire. Others are in turmoil with different types of wrong views. These are all causes of misery, therefore they are always painful like being on a precipice.

Gods suffer the misery of change. For example, signs of impending death and their fall to unfortunate states constantly oppress the minds of gods of the desire realm. How can they live in peace?

Pervasive misery is what arises under the power of causes characterized by actions and disturbing emotions. It has the nature and characteristics of momentary disintegration and pervades all wandering beings.

Therefore, see all wandering beings as immersed in a great fire of misery. Think that they are all like you in not desiring misery at all: 'Alas! All my beloved sentient beings are in such pain. What can I do to set them free?' and make their sufferings your own. Whether you are engaged in one-pointed meditation or pursuing your ordinary activities, meditate on compassion at all times, focusing on all sentient beings and wishing that they all be free from suffering.

Begin by meditating on your friends and relatives. Recognize how they experience the various sufferings that have been explained.

Then having seen all sentient beings as equal with no difference between them, you should meditate on sentient beings to whom you are indifferent. When the compassion you feel towards them is the same as the compassion you feel toward your friends and relatives, meditate on compassion for all sentient beings throughout the ten directions of the universe.

Just as a mother responds to her small, beloved and suffering child, when you develop a spontaneous and equal sense of compassion towards all sentient beings, you have perfected the practice of compassion. And this is known as great compassion.

Meditation on loving-kindness begins with friends and people you are fond of. It has the nature of wishing that they meet with happiness. Gradually extend the meditation to include strangers and even your enemies. Habituating yourself with compassion you will gradually generate a spontaneous wish to liberate all sentient beings. Therefore, having familiarized yourself with compassion as the basis, meditate on the awakening mind of bodhichitta.

X. Process of Meditation and its aspect and Focus

In the section called *Predicting the Magician Bhadra the Ratnakutika Sutra* states:

„These four are the compassions of a Bodhisattava. What are they? They are the compassion that delivers those that are born in the bad migration to the path of happy migration, the compassion that guides those with negative action to positive dharma, the compassion that makes those inclined towards lower path to greater path and the compassion that aspires to help all sentient beings thoroughly transcend suffering. Young man, moreover a bodhisattava sees there are sentient beings overpowered by pride, overpowered by great pride, overpowevered by pride of pride, overpowered by conceited pride, overpowered by manifest pride, overpowered by slight conceit, overpowered by wrong pride, thinking that I am higher than those lower than me, and viewing that I am more special than those equal to me. They accept the physical form as the self to accepting consciousness as the self. They feel they know which they do not know. Tthey do not say respectful words to those who are worthy of respectful words. They do not pay homage to those who are worthy of homage. They do not bow down to those that are elder and that are younger. They do not respect the seniors. They do not ask what is virtuous and what is nonvirtuous, what should be cultivated and what should not be cultivated, what is proper and what is improper, what is sinful and what is not sinful, what is path, what is meditative stabilisation and what is thorough liberation. To himself he will say I am the chief, I am supreme. When you see people acting with such conceitedness, show the path of truth, dharma, to help them discard all forms of pride. Thus a bodhisattava shows his compassion to sentient beings.

Young man, also a bodhisattava sees those who are without the influence of spiritual friends and surrounded by evil friends and who are therefore overpowered by by nonvirtuous friends and thus have developed attachment to nonvirtuous actions. Thus when a bodhisattava sees these beings taking life, stealing, engaging in sexual misconduct, lying, engaging in divisive talk, harsh speech, idle chatter, covetousness, harmful intention and wrong view. A bodhisattava shows the path of the truth so that they invite spiritual friends, stop the nonvirtuous path and uphold properly the path of ten virtuous actions. Thus a bodhisattava practices compassion to sentient beings."

Although all phenomena are selfless (having no intrinsic existence) but sentient beings do not show interest in selflessness. Therefore the Tathagatas develop compassion to sentient beings and so forth.

Alas! this wordly existence. Sentient beings are thoroughly influenced by mutual argument and enter the wrong way of harmful intention. In order to help them discard this, the Tathagata gives teaching. Thus the Tathagata develops great compassion to sentient beings.

XI. Relevance of compassion in today's world

Compassion is as relevant today as it was centuries ago. It is perhaps even more relevant and needed today. Until we succeed in changing ourselves into machines the need of compassion will always be there. Today's unchecked trend of hoarding and pursuing material goods from the limited natural resources is already proving suicidal. We have almost no knowledge of ourselves while we keep on exploring the external reality in great details. Unless you know yourself properly how can you take good care of yourself. I as a living human being have the need to take care both my body and my mind. We keep on feeding the body and have for so long starved the mind. If we need cross cultural understanding and brotherly and sisterly love and affection across the continents and oceans we should highlight and practice, not just talking, those qualities that we all share and cherish equally. Let us therefore not only feed the body but also nourish the mind with fundamental human good qualities, the basic spirituality, like compassion and wisdom which in Buddhism are seen as two wings of the bird to soar to the space of enlightenment and happiness. With wisdom you will not get stuck in the quagmire of narrow-minded fundamentalism and fanaticism that are rooted in blind egoism. And compassion will empower you to continuously develop and sustain the wish to care for suffering sentient beings, however much the difficulty may be. Atisha's Lamp of the Path says:

> Both compassion without wisdom
> And wisdom without compassion
> Is said to be a bondage
> Hence the wise ones should adopt both.

May all beings be happy. Sarva Mangalam

Tibetan sources referred:

1. Ratnakutika Sutra Volume Cha page 95
2. Ratnakutika Volume Ga Bodhisattavapitaka 144 Front page line 7
3. Ratnamegha Sutra Volumes Tsa page 77 back page line 2
4. Ratnamegha Sutra Volume Tsa page 78 front page line 6
5. Kamalashila's Stages of Meditation (Bhavanakram) Part 2
6. Fifth Dalai Lama's Word of Manjushri
7. Atisha's Lamp of the Path (Bodhipathpradipam)
8. Tsong Khapa's Great Stages of Meditation

4. Chapter

Compassion: Etymology, Rituals, Anecdotes from the Hindu Tradition

KUTUMBA SASTRY

T HE ESSENTIAL EXERCISE of any cross-cultural conversation is to study the similarities and dissimilarities between various schools of philosophies and cultures. In one sense it is tangible exercise and in other sense it is intangible. Because whether east or west, north or south, the core philosophical concepts and values remain the same. For example, it is inconceivable that any school of philosophy or culture can hold the position that there is no room for a concept/value called compassion in their tradition. The nature and the primacy of concept of compassion remain the same in all traditions. There cannot be any basic difference.

Yet, since language is the medium of expression and since each and every language has its own way of expression and specific limitations, efforts to strike one to one correspondence between concepts/values of various philosophies/cultures seldom stands to be futile. Yet, the exercise to study similarities and dissimilarities is very much relevant and need of the hour because such exercise alone will lead the mankind on right path to establish coherence and co-existence necessary for its own enlightenment and benefit.

I. Brief of Western Thinking

The term compassion constitutes two parts, namely, "com" and "passion." Com" means "collectively" and "passion" means "suffering." Combining both the meanings of two terms, the term "compassion" signifies "suffering collectively." In the Western tradition we have at least three terms, if not more, which appear to be synonyms. They are "compassion" "mercy" and "pity". The essential meaning of all the three remains the same as to "suffering collectively" or "suffering together with the other" or "a fellow feeling for the misery of others."

However, the distinction lies in the "added aspects" into the essential meaning. Pity is held to be "episodic" and hence "momentary." Therefore it is the lowest in the hierarchy. Relatively, compassion is higher and wider. It encompasses all fellow beings and lasts as long as one's life. It is a passion controlled by reason and virtue and hence "limited."

It involves several principles to further uphold its limited nature. For example: it involves the principles of "non-deserving", the principle of "commonality" and the principle of "proximity" to name a few. To explain the above principles: One gets compassion with respect to some fellow being only in the case where he has fallen prey to some suffering which he does not deserve.

That is if a criminal is punished under law in various ways, no one gets compassion about him even though he is also a "suffering fellow being." Similarly, to evoke compassion in someone's mind, there is a need for some or the other kind of "commonality" between the person who undergoes undeserving sufferance and the person who becomes compassionate towards him. Such commonality can be anything like common nation-hood, common habitat, common work place, common community so on and so forth.

The factor "proximity" overlaps with the factor of "commonality" to some extent. It can be any kind of "proximity" such as family, office, neighborhood etc. All the three factors also contribute towards increasing the degree of intensity of compassion. The idea of compassion comprises the idea of inequality and hence compassion is possible only between two 'unequal' fellow beings. Therefore it is clear that even though compassion is higher and wider in its nature, still it is 'limited' by several factors and principles.

For this very reason it cannot be absolute but remains a 'relative' concept. 'Mercy', on the other hand, is still higher and wider where principles of 'forgiveness' and 'justice' are involved and therefore stands to be 'unlimited' and 'absolute' concept. Mercy is possible between equals also. God can have only mercy but not compassion as he is totally free from any kind of suffering.

II. Brief of Hindu Thinking

In the tradition of Hinduism (Vedic Santana Dharma), several terms signifying the idea of compassion are available. Most important of them are again three in number and, in the first sight, they appear to be in correspondence with the three terms discussed above. These are Daya, Karuna and Anukampa. Even though we shall try to distinctively show the difference in the shades of meaning of the above terms in the following paragraphs, it may be noted that throughout sastraic and literary works all the three terms are used freely in an inter-changeable way. The Amarakosa, the traditional Sanskrit dictionary of synonyms, enumerates seven synonyms, namely, Karunya, Karuna, Ghrina, Kripa, Daya, Anukampa and Anukrosha. All the well known Sanskrit dictionaries, both the traditional and modern, do show all of them as synonyms and use the terms in an interchangeable way.

III. The Semantics of Compassion

The term Karuna is the derivative of root 'kri' added with Unadi suffix "unan." Therefore, its derivative meaning is "to place one's mind in others' favour" (karoti manah anukulyaya). Karuna is also one of the eight/nine sentiments enumerated by Bharatamuni. It is born of grief on account of loss or difficulties of near and dear. The term Daya is the derivative of root 'daya' added with suffix (an). It is defined as "the desire of one's bosom to mitigate the sorrow and difficulties of others by putting forth any amount of efforts[1]. It is also defined as "the action of remaining happy in treating all the living beings just as his own self for the benefit of their welfare and good." [2]

"Daya is to treat a stranger, a relative, a friend or foe as one's own self.[3]" "Daya is the realization of the fact that whatever is pleasing to one

---

[1] yatnadapi paraklesham hartum va hridi jayate/
iccha bhumisurashreshtha sa daya parikirtita//
—kriyayogasara, Padma Purana.

[2] atmavat sarva bhuteshu yo hitaya shubhaya ca/
vartate satatam hrishtah kriya hyesha daya smrita//
—Dahrmasutras of Gautama and also in the Matsyapurana.

[3] pare va bandhuvarge va mitre dveshtari va sada/
atmavad vartitavyam hi dayaisha parikirtita//

self should also be pleasing to all living beings. In short, to see similarity of one's own self with respect of all living beings[4].

From the definitions of daya and karuna it becomes clear that compassion in Hinduism is an attitude as well as a value. In Hindu tradition the aspect of "common suffering" seems to be absent as suffering is personal in Hindu tradition. All that it speaks about is to place oneself in the situation of other to realize the pain or pleasure the other person undergoes. Thus says the Bhagavadgītā. " He is the wise person who experiences all living beings as one's own self[5]."

The word "anukampā" is the derivative of root kapi which means 'moving or shivering gently.' The prefix anu gives the sense of 'following.' Thus putting together, the word means "to experience mild and gentle movement in the heart following the observance of pain and suffering in the other person."

The above definitions of a few important terms throw light on the nature of compassion as understood by the Indian tradition. When we put together the ideas expressed above, we derive almost a reasonable parallelism between western understanding of the concept and that of Indian understanding. The sum-substance of the definitions shown above stand parallel to the essential nature of compassion, mercy and pity discussed elsewhere. There appears to be some difference in understanding. For example, we have discussed a kind of hierarchy in respect of set of western terms/concepts which is not found in the Hindu terms.

The Principle of "non-deserving" may hold good with Indian tradition also as there cannot be compassion towards a person who deserves pain and suffering on any account. However, the principle of 'commonality' and 'proximity' are out-side the domain of compassion in Indian tradition as all the definitions shown above repeatedly speak about 'all living beings'(sarva bhutani). In one of the definition[6] "pare va" etc., all kinds of 'commonalities' and 'proximities' have been clearly negated.

As we have already pointed out in the previous pages, karunā is mostly defined in relation with pain, grief and suffering on account of loss of near

---

—Ekadashitattvam.
[4] manya yathatmanobhishtthah bhutanamapi te tatha/ atmaupamyena sarvatra dayam kurvanti sadhavah.
[5] atmavat sarva bhutani yah pashyati sa pashyati.
[6] See under note 3 above.

and dear etc. That is why it is specifically accepted as one of the nine sentiments in the same form. Soka (grief) is accepted as its sthāyibhāva. The first poetic master-piece, namely, the Rāmāyana is held to be the outcome of sharing of grief and sorrow of lady krauncha bird by the sage-author Valmiki when male krauncha bird was shot dead by a hunter. Accordingly, karuna is held to be the main sentiment in the Ramayana and soka or grief is its sthāyibhāva.

In contrast to this, the story of Sibi an Emperor of lunar race, stands as an illustration for Dayā . Sibi was an emperor with great qualities including daya in all living beings. One day a dove rushed to him and sought his refuge as it has been chasten by a kite. Soon after, the kite too arrived to him and argued with him that he is causing its death on account of lack food by giving shelter and refuge to its prey. As Sibi was compassionate towards all living beings, he found a way out by offering his flesh equal to the weight of dove to save both from their difficulties. Sibi's story is narrated in the Mahabharata[7].

Again there is a story of sage Dadhichi in the Mahabhārata roots of which go to the age of the Vedas. The Rakshasas waged a war with Indra under the leadership of Vritrāsura. Indra could not resist him and ultimately got defeated by him. Indra then approached Brahmā to know the way to kill Vritrāsura. Brahma advised him that spinal bones of Maharshi Dadhichi may come to his help. Indra then approached sage Dadhichi on the banks of river Saraswati along with Nara and Narāyana, and entreated him to part with his bones for the success of Devas in the war against Vritrāsura.

The sage Dadhichi readily welcomed the request and discarded his life from the body so that the entire lifeless body is put at disposal of Indra to collect bones and prepare Vajrāyudha with which later on he killed Vritrāsura.

Apart from the definitions of terms karunā and dayā, these above mentioned stories throw light on subtle nuances of difference in the use of words. It is also clear from the above that there is no human animal divide in conceiving the concepts karunā and dayā and neither one of them is restricted to the divine origin.

---

[7] Mahabharata, vanaparvan, chapter 197.

Further, karuṇā is predominantly an emotion where as dayā is predominantly an attitude/disposition. While karuṇā is a natural instinct dayā is a value that can be aquired and/or expanded. In fact, the term dayā and the term karuṇā. are used interchangeably.

Now, a few remarks on "collective suffering" from the point of view of Hinduism are in place in the context. Suffering is essentially personal. It can not be directly shared. The other persons can have "the feel" of someone's suffering on account of identifying themselves with the ones who are suffering. Common situations will help one to place oneself in the situation of other and undergo the experience of its resultant suffering. Therefore, there is no possibility of "collective suffering" but only "sharing of feeling or experience of others' suffering" is possible.

IV. The Eight Qualities of the Soul

The Dharmasūtras of Gautama, which is one of the very important prescriptive texts of code of conduct, speaks about eight qualities of the soul which are unavoidably essential to be fit to attain liberation. The very first of the list is Dayā. They are:

1. Dayā sarvabhūteshu (compassion towards all living beings,)
2. Kshāntih (forbearance)
3. Anasūya (lack of jealousy)
4. Saucha (Purity of money, mind, speech and body)
5. Anāyāsa (comfort, both physical and mental)
6. Mangala (to do virtuous deeds and to avoid non-virtuous deeds)
7. Akarpanya (composture not to seek help from others even while in great difficulties) and
8. Aspruha (lack of desire in all objects of senses)

Apart from these eight qualities (attributes) of soul, Gautama enumerates forty numbers of refinements (Sanskaras) in an elaborate way which are held to be essential to make oneself to be liberated. We do not want to discuss them for want of space.

At the end, Gautama observes that the one who possesses all the forty refinements of soul (samskaras) but does not possess the eight qualities of soul does not attain the liberation. On the other hand, the one who possesses all the eight qualities of the soul and possesses a few refinements (samskaras), even though not all forty, still attains liberation. From the discussion made above, the primacy of eight qualities of the soul is clear of which daya/ compassion stands in the foremost place. Therefore, according to Hinduism, whether one fulfils other conditions or not, one has to fulfill the condition of daya, (compassion) to make him fit for the liberation. Dayā as defined by Gautama is explained in the beginning of this paper[8].

V. Dynamics of Compassion

As part of forty refinements (samskaras) every house-holder is ordained to perform five rituals (sacrifices, yajnas) every day. They are called five great sacrifices (pancha mahayajnas)[9]. When we look into their nature we understand them to be very simple activities. But they are termed "great sacrifices", whereas other sacrifices that require great amount of money, strain, time and thousands and thousands of activities to perform are simply called "sacrifices" or yajnas . This itself gives an insight into the mind of writers on code of conduct in Hinduism.

The five mahayajnas (great sacrifices) are termed in sanskrit as Devayajna, Pitruyajna, Manushyayajna, Bhutayajna and Brahmayajna. All these five yajnas are to be performed everyday by the house-holder for life.

Devayajna (Sacrifice to Gods) is to do worship of one's God mainly offering some food as offering (naivedyam) along with other performances such as lighting a lamp before God etc.

Pitruyajna (Sacrifice to manes) is to offer water or water with sesame seeds to one's own manes such as father/mother etc. provided they are not alive. In case they are alive, some specified common manes are to be offered water.

Manushyayajna (Sacrifice to humans) is to feed the people who have reached the door-step of the house-holder every time he takes food.

Bhūtayajna (sacrifice to all living beings) is to offer food to birds, insects, watering plants etc. before taking food.

Brahmayajna (sacrifice to the rishis) is to recite at least one chapter from the Veda every day before taking food.

---

[8] See under note 2 above.
[9] "pancha va ete mahayajnah"
—Taittiriya Aranyaka 2.10

Hinduism believes that everyone and every living object should get some food to satisfy their hunger. And the house-holder has an obligation to discharge to see that everyone is happy. The basis for this obligation is compassion towards all living beings. Further, the philosophy behind these rituals is to pay back something to the parties from whom we receive our life and growth. We get food on account of grace of God through rains and crops, we derive our life on account of our forefathers and we also produce our food on account of animals and plants. Therefore, some part of food prepared for ourselves be parted with the above. Otherwise we equate ourselves with thieves and robbers.

Hinduism believes in Karma theory and rebirth. According to it one reaps the fruits as one sows them. No one can alter one's the course of one's own life whether joyful or sorrowful and painful. One has to undergo the life as it is given on account of his/her own past deeds. Therefore, compassion is not to mitigate the pain and sorrow of others but to remain concerned about it.

Bhagavadgita states clearly thus: "The one who eats alone without parting a part to those from whom he received it is none but a thief[10]." Even the first book of the world, namely, the Rigveda states that, "The one who eats alone eats only the sin."[11]

The philosophical and religious thinking has been fully translated into action in Hinduism. Sometimes we do not understand the significance of some prescriptions until we know the basic philosophical thinking underlying them. For example: Every Hindu is prescribed to put rangoli (a design containing circles, squares, lines etc to make a combination of flowers, shapes and forms) right in the front of entry to the house on the bare ground. In good olden days the front court-yard used to be only in clay. (Unlike cemented now a days). And the rangoli put on the floor is done with rice or wheat (unlike now-a-days where people use chemical colors). The significance behind this prescribed activity is compassion towards lesser living beings such as ants, insects etc. Even now, in most parts of In-

---

[10] "taitdattanapradayaibhyo yo bhunkte stena eva sah"
—Bhagavadgita.
[11] "kevalagho bhavati kevaladi"
—Rigveda.

dia, especially in south India people put it every day ritualistically. Most people consider the absence of it as in-auspicious.

VI. Ahimsa and Compassion

The concept ahimsā can also be considered as the dynamic aspect of compassion. We can relate compassion and ahimsā with cause-and-effect relation. As is well known, Hinduism gives great importance to the concept of ahimsā in all the texts on religion and philosophy. Indian culture and history stand in attestation to the primacy, commitment and dedication to the concept of ahimsā.

There existed a long line of crusaders of ahimsā in India from time immemorial to the recent past – the age of Mahatma Gandhi. I do not want to elaborate on this for obvious reasons. However, one has to be very careful to understand the Hindu mind with regard to what they understand by the word ahimsā. Hindus were very clear that himsā or injury is unavoidable to carry on life for any species. In addition, humanity is ordained to commit injury to fellow being and living organisms while cultivating land, preparing food and discharging various other activities.

Various professions like to be a king to rule a country, or to be scientists and carry out various experiments on humans and animals, preparation of medicines, containing the over growth of certain poisonous species and wild life, butchery etc. compel people to cause injury to others unavoidably. Similarly a person engaged in discharging Vedic injunctions is also ordained to cause injury to the sacrificial animals. If you extend this observation to the level of bacterial and cell mutation level, every other moment we are committing injury to some living form unavoidably and to some extents without our agency. Therefore, non-injury (ahimsa) in totality is impossibility. Therefore, the concept of ahimsa (non-injury) has to be understood as bounded with various limitations. The purpose of above discussion is not to speak about ahimsa but to highlight the Hindu point of view of acting upon compassion. Let us see how it happens.

There is a ritual, namely, "Vaishvadeva" which is performed through offering some specified objects in fire prepared and lit through a specific process before taking food. Every house holder has to do it from the day he gets married till he breaths last. This ritual is prescribed as a measure to do away with the sin that a person commits unavoidably as we have explained above. Five kinds of such sins have been identified to do away which the "Vaishvadeva" ritual is prescribed in the Yajurveda. So, this tradition is in existence from the Vedic age.

The five sins are: injury caused to various kinds of living beings by oven, crushing stone, broomstick, pounding instruments and water pot[12]. This ritual is elaborated in the Devibhagavata skandha 11 also. After finishing "Vaishvadeva", "gograsa" offering rice to cow should also be done.

For a believer in the ritual it is to ward off the sins committed unavoidably. For a non-believer as well as believer it should be construed as showing compassion towards lesser-life forms against which injury is caused, though in an unavoidable way.

Similarly, every time a householder takes food, little amount of water is dropped from hand in the plate before washing hand. This water is meant for them who are placed in the hell for millions and millions of years on account of their bad-deeds. Well, the water may not reach them, but this action certainly refines the mind of the eater and fills his heart with compassion towards most condemnable sinners.

It reminds everyone at every time of eating food about his duty towards those sinners by bringing them to the conscious mind of the eater. In the same way, during annual death ceremony of elders there is an elaborate ritual when food is offered to the parents and other elders who have passed away as well as to all those who served them in any humble capacity. All the above mentioned rituals and sacrifices are continuously being performed by great number of people in Hindu tradition even today. Therefore, compassion in Hinduism is not only in preaching but also in everyday rituals that are performed. In other words, not only he parents but all living beings from insects onwards to animals and plants, from most condemnable sinners and servants are shown due concern and compassion by a house-holder by performing the rituals everyday and every time he eats food. It is not possible to discuss all the practices that show concern and compassion towards one's own kith and kin, neighbors when they are in pain and sorrow.

---

[12] "pancha suna grihasthasya chulli peshanyupaskarah/
kandani chodakumbhashca badhyate yastu vahayan//
tasam kramena sarvasam nishkrityartham maharshibhis/
pancha klipta mahayajnah pratyaham grihamedhinam//
—Manusmriti 3.68–69

This karma and rebirth theory absolves God, to a large extent, as not being compassionate and cruel towards those who undergo various sorrows and pains during their life. Thus to be compassionate is not to mitigate the sorrow and pain of others, but only to remain supportive.

VII. Conclusion

1. Compassion is a value and/or attitude rather than a mere feeling or emotion.
2. Some prefer the Sanskrit term Daya, some Karuna to denote compassion.
3. There is no clear cut division between compassion and mercy.
4. Compassion is partly natural and partly to be cultivated.
5. It is an absolute concept because it is shown towards most sinners, too. It is also relative because it is shown in greater degree towards good people in pain and suffering.
6. It has no dichotomy with himsa if such himsa is unavoidable and enjoined.
7. It is both limited as well as unlimited. Limited because unavoidable and enjoined himsa acts as limitation to it. Unlimited because it is shown towards most sinners and to the objects of unavoidable and enjoined himsa, too.
8. It is essentially an attitude and concern to be experienced and shown than to undertake action to mitigate the pain and sorrow of others. However, wherever possible it results in such actions.
9. Sufferance is personal and hence collective sufferance is not possible.
10. Commonality and proximity may cause increase in its degree, but it is universal in its nature.
11. There is no divine or human divide in its experience and/or expression.
12. It is the first and foremost of eight atmagunas (qualities of soul).
13. It is effective only when it is translated into action.
14. For most of prescriptions in the books on code of conduct, compassion acts as their basis and goal.

5. Chapter

"Have we not all one Father?" Toward a Psychohistory of the Jewish Idea of Compassion

BOB CARROLL

THE GOAL OF THIS PAPER is to explore the theological, textual, and intellectual bases for the idea of compassion in Judaism, to discuss how it was applied in Jewish history, and consider the forces which have led, in various historical periods, to it being applied either restrictively or expansively in regard to the degree of commitment that the Jew is supposed to have towards the betterment of humanity as a whole. In doing so we would be remiss if we did not consider the role of human psychology as well. So it is fitting that we begin our discussion with a few words about how people approach religious texts and religious ideas and how their affiliation with their religious communities leads them to view those who are outside of their own camp.

Gandhi, in the introduction to his autobiography, noted that "The world crushes the dust under its feet, but the seeker after truth should so humble himself that even the dust could crush him" (Gandhi 1993: XV) It seems to me that this essential humility is the defining element in any authentically spiritual personality, and many Jewish thinkers, especially within the mystical tradition, have expressed the very same thought – indeed the book of Genesis (28:14) tells us that "Thy seed shall be as the dust of the earth", which is understood by one of the medieval commentators, Obadia ben Jacob Sforno, to mean that "only after your seed has reached the lowest depths of misery and degradation and is treated like the very dust of the earth will salvation come [...]"[1] – in other words, only once Israel

---

[1] Translated in Cohen (1947: 165).

has experienced degradation and humility can its true spiritual nature be manifest. Our own experiences in history are supposed to be practica in how to feel empathy for others in similar circumstances – "You shall love the stranger for you were strangers in the Land of Egypt" (Deuteronomy 10:19).

But sometimes religion does not succeed in instilling such a sense of compassion towards others. Indeed, we live in an age when all religions are in danger of being taken over by fanatics, who not only succumb to xenophobia but even, sometimes, consciously elevate it to the status of an ideological principle.[2] So our task is not to take the easy way out – to simply underscore the many statements within Judaism and in all religions that emphasize compassion, decency, and tolerance, but also to ask ourselves the hard questions: why is it that for some people religious belief constricts and blunts their compassion and replaces it with unfeeling judgmentalism? I am not necessarily speaking here of extremists. All religious communities have them, and it's easy to tell ourselves that each group has some fanatics and misanthropes in it. But it would be more honest, as well as more difficult, to admit to ourselves that even many mainstream adherents of all religions seem to have become people with shriveled little souls and cold hearts. We need to ask hard questions of ourselves as religious people. Religion makes great use of the idea of compassion but so often fails to train its adherents to act compassionately. How does one catalyze a person to both feel compassion and to act upon it, and why is it that attempts to inculcate a sense of compassion so often fail?

Let's think about this for a moment from the point of view of psychoanalysis. What is a fanatic? To my mind, a fanatic is a person who thinks in black and white, who denies the legitimacy of any other views besides his own. Who derives comfort from the certainty that there is no value in anything or anyone outside of his own group, and who responds to anything that challenges his faith with rage and hatred. Who confuses extremism for authenticity and conformity for piety, thus subverting the open-ended search for religious truth to blind obedience to prejudice or external authority.

---

[2] For a series comprehensive studies of how fanatic and fundamentalist mindsets are manifest in various present-day religious communities, the reader is referred to Marty and Appleby (1994).

In psychoanalytic terms, what I am speaking about is reminiscent of what is known in the literature as the latency period in child development – This is a period between the ages of about six to pre-teen (ages 12–13). "In the latency period", modern psychology teaches us, "the average child settles down, enjoys structure, understands that authority is in charge and gets pleasure in performing the good tasks that teachers require. *During latency pleasure is derived by compliance*" (Banschick 2009). And the result of carrying over this sort of thinking into adulthood is, unsurprisingly, exactly what we find in preteen societies: cliques. Cliques operate according to rigid social rules, and group consensus functions as an authority which legislates what is right or wrong, fashionable or unacceptable. Regarding the infantilizing effects of abuse of authority in religious practice, we often need look no farther than the clergy of a latency-minded faith community. If you to live your life bound by a cocoon of certainty and rigid norms of behavior, this is easily found within all faiths.

This infantilized version of religion reduces spiritual life into a projection of ultimate authority on a figure like God, or worse – on religious leaders – who in turn tell their followers what to do in order to be acceptable. Followers become empowered only through identification with the leadership or with God himself. At its most extreme form this manifests itself in mass suicides by cult members, or the terrorist who becomes convinced that he is obeying God by destroying the lives of himself and others. A less dramatic example is the parishioner who reveres his pastor, rabbi or imam or priest as the final word on all things personal, no matter how minute, and no matter how destructive of his personal autonomy. This authoritarianism and cliquishness, when manifested in religious communities or translated into religious ideology, leads to devaluation or even demonization of anyone who questions the group's values or adheres to a different belief system. The tendency to believe that one's own group contains the whole truth and other religions are pure falsehood thus results from the "latency" mode of thinking.

With these issues in mind, let us now examine some core Jewish texts that impinge on this discussion, and think about how they were applied during the course of Jewish history. Several lively discussions have been recorded in Jewish literature over which verse of the Bible encapsulates, as it were, the core teachings of Judaism or sums up all of Jewish teaching in one line. The Jerusalem Talmud records such a debate between Rabbi

Akiva, one of the most influential figures in the development of Rabbinic law and ethics, and Ben Azzai (Jerusalem Talmud, Tractate Nedarim, ch. 9, p. 60, author's translation). Rabbi Akiva's position is very well known: he says that the verse which sums up all of Judaism is "Love Your neighbor as yourself" (Leviticus 19:18). But Ben Azzai, on the other hand, offers a seemingly strange competing candidate for the one verse which sums up the whole Law: "This is the book of the generations of man [...]" This suggestion seems rather puzzling, until we realize that Ben Azzai was incompletely quoting Genesis 5:1: "This is the book of the generations of man; in the day that God created man, in his image he created him." How can we understand this dispute, and why did Ben Azzai not think that Akiva's view, which seems so self-evident and which has been so beloved in our history, was acceptable?

Upon reflection, we note that there are two possible limitations with the verse Rabbi Akiva suggested: One, it makes the commandment to love be dependent on a subjective feeling – how much, or whether, one loves oneself. And perhaps more obviously, it restricts the commandment to love to one's neighbor – however we define it. For the medieval commentators on this page of Talmud, that was seen as being a fatal flaw, because it means that it is possible to interpret Rabbi Akiva's principle non-universally. Ben Azzai's verse, on the other hand, states, as it has been understood by Rabbinic teaching, that all human beings are of infinite worth and have an essential claim on our ethical concern by dint of being created in the Divine image. For him, the doctrine of each human being being in the "Image of God" furnishes us with a conceptual umbrella which of necessity includes all human beings at all times and all places. For this reason, it is possible to say that Ben Azzai's verse is a logical pre-requisite of Rabbi Akiva's, since without it, our ethics would ultimately be based on subjective feelings alone, and the scope of our ethical concern may be defined restrictively, to apply only to certain groups of people, or only under certain conditions. Rabbinic Judaism was profoundly uncomfortable with such a possibility, and strove instead to build a conceptual model which proves that all human beings, in all places and of all religions or beliefs, are of equal – infinite – worth and have an inalienable ethical claim upon us. This is part of Judaism's answer, if correctly and fully understood, to latency religion, or fanaticism, or cliquishness or whatever one wants to call it, which leads to valuing only those who conform or are part of one's own group.

Let's look at a few more passages which explore different facets of this principle.

Especially important is a passage from the Mishna, the foundational work of rabbinic law (Tractate Bava Kama ch. 8 Mishna 6, author's translation), wherein the very same Rabbi Akiva emphasizes that even if a person does not show respect for her or his own dignity, that does not permit less respect on our part towards him. This is so because, as Rabbi Tanhuma states elsewhere (Sifra 4:12, author's translation) and as we have already learned above, any act which dishonors a human being is an act of disrespect to God Himself, precisely because "In his image he created him (mankind)."

One of the most powerful passages in all of Talmudic literature is the admonition given by the judges of a rabbinic court to witnesses in capital cases, cases where the accused may in theory be put to death for murder or another capital crime (Tractate Sanhedrin ch. 4 Mishna 5, author's translation). The reader should note that by the time the Mishna was written and redacted, in 200 CE, Jewish courts no longer had capital jurisdiction – so the discussion was purely theoretical. But listen to how the rabbis use the oppportunity to teach us a profound ethical point:

"Know", the judges would say, "that capital cases are not like civil cases [...] for in civil cases (if the defendant is wrongly convicted on the basis of false testimony) he (the witness) may make financial restitution and thus atone. But in capital cases, if the accused is wrongly killed, his blood and that of all his descendants through all eternity are upon the one who testified against him." "For that reason," the text continues, the Bible teaches us that "one single human being, (Adam) was created by God." After all, God could just as easily have created a whole race, or at least a man and woman together at the same time. Why then did he create Adam alone?

The rabbis explain that by creating a single human being who was the progenitor of all humanity, God intended to teach us that "One who destroys one person's life, it is considered as if he destroyed a whole world, and he who preserves on person's life, it is as if he has preserved a whole world [...] And to declare the greatness of the Holy One Blessed be He, for when a human person mints coins from the one mold they all appear identical, but the Holy One Blessed be He "minted" every person from the

mold of the first human being, but not one is identical to another. Therefore a person should say, the 'world was created for my sake.' And also: so
no one can (be a racist) and say "My father was greater than your father."
Because in Adam we all have the same father. The Hebrew word for "human being" is simply "ben adam" – a child of Adam. And as every human
being is created in God's image, we have no right to read anyone out of the
circle of human compassion. Every life is infinitely, and equally, precious
as a microcosm and representative of all humanity.

We see, in these core texts of the Rabbinic/Talmudic tradition, a strong
theoretical basis for extending compassion to all peoples. The knowledge
that we are all children of Adam was intended, say the Rabbis, to compel
us to think and live in a manner which recognizes actual familial bonds.
In this scheme, any act of compassion towards another human being is
an expression of genuine sibling devotion, and to murder or to allow any
human being to perish because of our own inaction is fratricide. It is worth
commenting that the very first prayer which the Bible records is that of
Abraham, the first Jew, praying for the sinners of the evil city of Sodom
(Genesis 18:16–33) – a city whose men devoured each other; a group of
people who could not be more alien, in terms of belief and actions, from
what the Bible approves of. Yet Abraham argues even with God himself to
have compassion on them and spare their lives.

Over the course of the centuries, some have argued, often in the context
of anti-Jewish polemics, that Judaism is a dry, legalistic religion that does
not seek to imbue its followers with a true sense of compassion. This claim
cannot survive even a casual glance at the body of Judaism's teachings,
from the Torah (the first five books of the Bible) to the Prophetic books
and the vast body of Rabbinic lore. True, Judaism is a religion of law and
obligation. True, as we have seen, the rabbis were uncomfortable making
our obligations toward others depend on a subjective feeling which may
change or which may not include all people. But the language of obligation
is simply the legal way of expressing the theological idea that all human beings are divinely precious, and therefore possess inherent rights. "Justice",
to quote the late Dr. AJ Heschel, "[...] is an interpersonal relationship, implying both a claim and a responsibility [...] The necessity of submitting to
a law is derived from the necessity of identifying with what concerns other
individuals or the whole community of men. Justice is valid because of the
community that unites all individuals" (Heschel 1969: 209–210). Compas-

sion is a statement that justice needs to be done; an assertion of human empathy, concern, and community. Yet for Judaism, ultimately compassion is a feeling, whereas justice is a demand, and an obligation, based on the religious idea that each human being is divinely precious. The obligation exists irrespective of whether the subjective feeling of compassion or empathy is present.

More broadly speaking, we are taught that a person is not merely obligated to do what the legal system mandates as a minimum, because no legal system, no matter how comprehensive, can possibly foresee every situation. Judaism addresses this issue by describing God as a compassionate God whom we, in order to become more Godly beings, must imitate. In the beginning of the book of Exodus, we are taught that God heard the cry of the Israelites in bondage, and was moved to liberate them (Exodus 3:7). Similar expressions of divine pathos occur in many other places. Talmudic Judaism concretized imitation of God's compassion as a binding ethical value in this manner, as described in the Talmud (Tractate Sotah, 14A, Author's translation):

> "What is the meaning of the verse 'After the Lord they God thou shalt walk?' Is it possible for a human being to walk after the Divine presence? Is it not written, 'For the Lord your God is a consuming fire?' Rather it means to follow after God by imitating his actions. Just as he clothes the naked, as it is written, 'And the Lord made for the man and his wife coats of skin, and he clothed them' – so too, you should clothe the naked. The Holy One, Blessed Be he, visited the sick, as it is written, 'And the Lord appeared to Abraham by the oak trees of Mamre (after he had been circumcised).' So too, you should visit the sick. The Holy One, Blessed be He, comforts mourners, as it is said, 'And it came to pass, after the death of Abraham, that God blessed Isaac his son'. So you too, comfort mourners. The Holy One, Blessed be He, buries the dead, as it is written, 'And he buried him (Moses) in the valley.' So you too, bury the dead."

Despite the centrality of this teaching in Rabbinic Judaism – indeed, perhaps because of it – there is no single Hebrew translation for the English word "compassion." Perhaps the closest word is "rachamim", often translated as mercy, and which is from the same Hebrew root as the word "rechem", or womb. In this model, God's motherly love for her children would thus be the model for human compassion. Another possibility is the word "chessed", usually translated as lovingkindness, a phrase which figures prominently in a Biblical passage which has a central place in Jewish liturgy: "Merciful God, merciful God, powerful God, compassionate and gracious, slow to anger, and abundant in lovingkindness and truth" (Exodus 34:6–7). This passage is recited by every Jew on every major Jewish festival and on the High Holy Days, as a means of acknowledging God's abundant compassion and asking for his mercy despite our manifold human failings and sins.

Let's take a moment to analyze what the above passages, as a whole, tell us. Religion, for Judaism, is not about an escape from this world into heavenly realms, or about establishing an individual relationship with God that has no ethical purpose.[3] Other human beings are not a detour on the road to God; they *are* the road (Buber 1983: 30–33). Judaism doesn't in any way denigrate the importance of individual religious experience; we have a vast literature from Jewish mystics and spiritual seekers, some of which will be presented later in this paper. But Judaism did seek to radically transform the purpose and meaning of individual religious experience, expanding the divine-human encounter to include other human beings as well. For the Biblical prophets, this meant that prophetic inspiration or revelation occurs for the benefit of a 3rd party; its ultimate purpose is not primarily to offer comfort or individual illumination but rather to expand and intensify a person's ethical commitment to other human beings – for it is in upholding the value and dignity of human life, the prophets tell us, that a Jew properly worships God. Listen to the prophet Isaiah, in Chapter 58, which is read in every synagogue on Jewish fast days:

> "Behold, in the day of your fast you pursue business, and exact payments. You fast for strife and enmity, and smite with the fist of wickedness. You fast not to make your voice heard on high. Is this the fast that I have chosen? A day for one to afflict the soul, to bow the head like a bulrush and lie upon sackcloth and ashes like a mourner? You call this a fast, a day acceptable to the Lord? This is what I call a fast: unlock the shackles of your selfishness, and break the yoke of your greed. Free the oppressed, and break every bond; share your bread with the hungry and open your house to the homeless. When you see the naked, cover him; Protect the vulnerable. And turn not your back on your own flesh and blood" (Author's translation).

Ritual behavior easily becomes false. It can become sanctimonious and self-righteous, and can fill a person with self-satisfaction and a condescending spirit. This is spiritual poison. The Talmud tells us that no human face elicits the image of God himself in the heart of a human being more than the face of poverty, for when we look into the eyes of a poor person

---

[3] For a fuller explication of this point by a centrally important modern Jewish thinker, see Soloveitchik (1983: 30–33).

we see his vulnerability, and know the interrelatedness of all humanity.[4] So it is this particular image of God which, in its suffering, awakens our own innate Godliness by arousing our compassion and empathy.

The prophet Jeremiah writes in the same vein (Jeremiah 22:12–16):

> "Woe to him who builds his house with unrighteousness, and his rooms by injustice; who uses his neighbors service without wages, and gives him nothing for his work; that says, I will build me a huge house with large upper chambers, and cuts himself out windows, and covers it with rafters of cedar, and paints it with vermillion. Do you think that you will reign because you compete in cedar? Did not your father eat and drink, and do justice and righteousness, and then it was well with him? He judged the cause of the poor and needy, then it was well with him – is this not to know Me?"

One knows God by imitating his ways – by engaging in acts of compassion. Ritual acts without this consciousness are hypocritical at best. In Jewish liturgy, the sabbath and hoilidays are all described as reminders and remembrances of the Jewish people's exodus from slavery in Egypt. Why? Because it was the Exodus which proved that God hears our cries, and it was the Jewish people's experience of oppression in Egypt which is supposed to sensitize us to the plight of others.[5] Many Jewish ritual observances and holiday observances are re-imagined in light of this idea. Thus even the Sabbath, originally described as a remembrance of God's resting on the seventh day after he had finished the work of creation (Genesis 2:2–3), is additionally understood in the liturgy as being a commemoration of the Exodus from Egypt.[6]

As we know, the story of the Exodus, that unknown incident in the lifespan of a tiny people, became one of the most important tales in the history of mankind, and the centerpiece of the Bible, one of the most influential books in history. I think this is so because, paradoxically, it was this event, which crystallized our identity as a unique and separate nation, that also pointed to more universal significance. Slavery is the most extreme possible form of the oppression and misery under which most people have always lived. And, of course, the God who took the Israelites out of Egypt

---

[4] See Babylonian Talmud, Tractate Bava Batra, 10A: "When someone gives a coin to a poor person, he merits to see the face of the Divine Presence, as it is said: 'Through righteousness I will see your face' (Psalm 17:15)".

[5] See Deuteronomy 10:19: "You shall love the stranger, for you were strangers in the land of Egypt".

[6] See for example Birnbaum (1949: 289).

is also the God of Genesis, who created the universe and all of humanity, the children of Adam, and who taught us that the most fundamental teaching of religion is that all human life is of infinite worth by dint of being created in His image.[7]

So the fact that redemption came to Israel proves that God can one day bring redemption to the whole world – in other words, Messianic redemption for all peoples – the goal of history – is, as Rabbi Irving Greenberg very elegantly put it, "the Exodus writ large" (Greenberg 1988: 35). Someday, we are taught, humanity will live as if it fully recognizes the core Biblical message that we are all Images of God. It is our task in history to propagate this ideal and eventually bring it about. Doing so, of course, would be a revolutionary change in all aspects of human life: after all, what would it mean if we truly put this principle into practice and set it up as the primary goal of human society? It would mean than no one could ever go without medical care, or adequate food, or housing. It would mean that every child would have a right to education. It would mean that workers in the developing world could never be exposed to toxins for the benefit of multinational corporations, or work for barely subsistence wages. It would mean that social justice, not profits, would guide both our economic and political lives. This is truly a revolutionary goal: bringing about a genuine utopia on earth. But Judaism, which allowed in Biblical law even a very limited form of slavery, doesn't require us to bring about such a utopia all at once – one might say that the Bible and Talmud use evolutionary methods to achieve revolutionary goals. With the Exodus, God didn't yet bring final redemption, either to the Jewish people or to the world. What he did was to set up an ideal conception of what human life and human civilization are supposed to be. Slavery and oppression are never right or proper; they are not man's natural state. Inequality is not something ordained by God but a state of imperfection and which we must all work to overcome. This is a recurring theme in Jewish thought: It is up to us to become partners with God by imitating his attributes of compassion to repair and perfect the world. As Joseph Soloveitchik, a pre-eminent modern Orthodox Jewish thinker, wrote: "When God created the world, he provided an opportunity for the work of his hands – man – to participate in

---

[7] For a fuller exposition of this idea see Greenberg (1988: 34–39).

His creation. The Creator, as it were, impaired reality in order that mortal man could repair its flaws and perfect it" (Soloveitchik 1983: 101).

Now that we have spoken about the theoretical foundations of the idea of compassion in Judaism, let us return to an issue which we hinted at earlier – the tension which exists within the Jewish psyche between concern for ourselves and our own survival, affected as it was by the many vicissitudes and hardships of Jewish history, vs. the universalist thrust we spoke of earlier.

The development and application of any system of religious law does not occur in a vacuum, divorced from the needs and influences of real religious communities or immune to historical and psychological influences. In the case of Judaism, we see here a paradox: One the one hand, it was the Exodus from Egypt which gave the Jews their identity as a separate nation – what the Bible calls "a people that shall dwell alone, and shall not be counted among the nations" (Numbers 23:9). On the other hand, the message of the Exodus, and of the biblical and rabbinic teachings we have discussed earlier, are profoundly universalist, and Israel is also charged with the task of being a "light unto the nations" (Isaiah 42:6–7) by being the bearer of this Divine teaching throughout history.

But the Jewish people had to survive as a tiny oppressed minority, in exile from their land and often without political or legal rights, for 2000 years. It would be absurd and dishonest to suggest that this experience has not had a profound effect on the Jewish consciousness and on Jewish teachings. In later Talmudic times, the principle of "Love your neighbor as yourself" did in fact come to be interpreted restrictively – "neighbor" having been defined, despite the violence this did to the plain scriptural meaning, as referring to "one's neighbor in the commandments" – in other words, only a fellow Jew.[8] And "the stranger in your midst" was at times defined as referring only to what Talmudic law calls a "Ger Toshav", i.e., a convert to Judaism.[9] But in later medieval times, these restrictions were reversed by Menachem ha Meiri, who flourished in the late 13th and 14th centuries, and who taught that "nations restricted by the ways of religion", which meant the Christians in the midst of whom he lived as well as all other nations who possessed a code of moral conduct, were considered to

---

[8] See Simon (1975: 32–36).
[9] Ibid., 34.

be the same as Jews in all respects with regard to our ethical obligations toward them.[10] Meiri was followed by many other modern exegetes, such as Jacob Zvi Mecklenburg (1785–1865) who wrote that "Love your neighbor as yourself" means plainly that whatever good things one would like to have done to him by his neighbor, "he should do to his neighbor, *who is every human being.*"

Interestingly, certain modern academic scholars of Judaism have understood these changes as introducing ""new categories and conceptual structures into the law" in response to moral discomfort with the law as they found it in their own day, or as an attempt to read their contemporary moral sense back onto the ancient Jewish sources.[11] But it can readily be seen that these changes represent not a new imperative but rather a conscious return to the earlier Biblical/Rabbinic teachings which were infused with the awareness that each human being is a child of Adam, and an image of God, and that all are thus "neighbors" in his eyes.

This is perhaps a good place to note that, entirely aside from the phenomenon of changed historical circumstances calling forth new exegeses of biblical texts, Judaism has also always posited that there are circumstances when our obligation to show compassion is limited, or even perhaps immoral. We are taught, for example, that "He who is compassionate to the cruel will ultimately be cruel to the compassionate" (Midrash Tanchuma Metzora 1, Author's translation). The continuation of the same Mishnaic text we cited earlier about capital cases also records a view which says that court that sentences even one person to death in 70 years is considered to be a court of murderers, but also contains a dissenting opinion which argues that such leniency will only increase the shedders of blood within the nation. Yet even in cases where Biblical law enjoins us to show no mercy, rabbinic teaching frequently derived ethical lessons of a dramatically different sort by locating within the text itself issues and problems which the law presented therein did not explicitly purport to solve. A particularly compelling example of this sort of exegesis is the case of a city which has been led astray to worship other gods, in which case the Bible tells us "You shall smite the inhabitants of that city with the edge of the sword [...] so

---

[10] Ibid., 47–50.
[11] Ibid., 51.

that God will turn back from his burning wrath; and he will give you mercy and be merciful and multiply you" (Deuteronomy 13:16–18).

Commenting on this passage, Rabbi Chaim Ibn Atar, an influential medeival student of the Bible and renowned rabbinic decisor, was struck by the seeming redundancy of the language "[...] he will give you mercy and be merciful". In his commentary on the Pentateuch "Or haChaim" (Venice, 1742)[12] he interprets this dual language to mean that there are times when we have no choice but to commit acts which are cruel in nature in order to insure the survival of our nation. But such acts, even when performed in obedience to an explicit Divine command, carry with them a profound spiritual danger: they blunt our sense of mercy and destroy our sensitivity to human suffering. This, according to Ibn Atar, is why the Biblical texts says that God will "give you mercy" – this phrase teaches us that God will give us back the attribute of mercy which our experience, however necessary and even commanded, may well have extirpated from our hearts. I do not mean to evade the problematics of such commandments in the Bible, which trouble our moral sense very greatly. The point I am trying to make is that the teachers of classical Judaism were troubled by them as well, and sought ways to mitigate their effects, both by restricting their applicability and by warning us about the consequences of their performance. Rabbi Ibn Atar concludes by noting that "God will only have mercy upon one who himself is merciful", thus underscoring the danger of falling prey, as it were, to one's own cruelty, and deriving an ethical lesson from this disturbing Biblical passage which emphasizes the profound danger in subverting our sense of compassion for any reason, even – perhaps especially – at the behest of a divine command.

As in the above passage, we see a paradox, or a dialectical tension, in Judaism as a whole, which is manifest both historically and exegetically. A great deal of Jewish life and Jewish law are geared to providing for our survival as a separate people. Yet as we have seen the fundamental message of Judaism is deeply universal and deeply linked with concern for the welfare of the whole world.

It seems natural to think of these two thrusts, universalism (concern about all mankind) and particularism (concern primarily with our own well-being and survival) as being mutually opposed. One would think that

---

[12] *Mikraot Gedolot*, New York 1974, 176–177.

to the extent that one becomes inner-directed one loses a strong sense of being able to speak to, and learn from, the rest of humanity. And it seems intuitively true that those who are more concerned with the universalist aspects would reject a strong emphasis on our own particularist concerns. Indeed, Jewish history has borne this out. The early German Jewish reformers spoke of the expulsion of the Jews from their land as being a positive thing, a natural historical step which enabled the Jewish nation to fulfill its universalist mission to teach that all human beings are Images of God. For this reason they saw the modern Zionism as a step backward, a retreat into less lofty, more primitive nationalistic values. [13] But in emphasizing the universalist elements of Jewish teaching to the detriment of those practices and commandments which were intended to safeguard the physical survival of the Jewish people in history, the Reform camp placed that survival at risk. Jewish Orthodoxy, on the other hand, which clung to the Law and its staunch commitment to Jewish literacy and ritual observance, has been vastly more successful at passing itself along. But this has come at a steep price, namely the risk of being so inward-looking that children are raised to think and live in a self-perpetuating sociological bubble, which sees little value in nor seeks to contribute to the ennobling of humanity as a whole. This exclusive self-concern often leads to xenophobia or worse – racism and denigration of the Other.

But I would like to suggest that ultimately this is a false dichotomy. After all: if the deepest and most fundamental message of the Bible is that we must know that all human beings are the Image of God, then it follows that the particulars of Biblical, and indeed Jewish, teaching must serve this goal and be interpreted in a way which conforms with it. This understanding was taught by many prominent Jewish thinkers and especially mystics

---

[13] The Reform Movement's Philadelphia Conference of Nov. 3–6, 1869, adopted the following among its principles: "The messianic goal of Israel is not the restoration of the old Jewish state under a descendent of David, involving a second separation from the nations of the earth, but the union of all men as the children of God in the confession of the all embracing unity of God, so as to realize the unity of all rational creatures and their call to moral sanctification [...] We look upon the destruction of the second Jewish commonwealth not as a punishment for the sinfulness of Israel, but as a result of the divine purpose revealed to Abraham, which, as has become ever clearer in the course of the world's history, consists in the dispersion of the Jews to all parts of the earth, for the realization of their high-priestly mission, to lead the nations to the true knowledge and worship of G-d", see Temkin (1974: 39).

ntrolled by a broader ethical purpose, it can cease to be a positive
nd become poisonous. This form of nationalism must therefore be
nded:

> wever, when [...] (the national aspect) has succeeded in taking possession of the
> n, it expands and becomes fortified and acquires for itself a complete being [...]
> at times, even seeks to detach itself from its basic root, the content of the divine
> " (Kook 1961: 103, translated in Belfer 1995: 262). "The ultimate goal [...] is not just
> emarcate an isolated national entity, but to (bring about) the yearning to unite
> umanity into one family [...] and although this (ultimate goal) also requires a
> ial center, the intention is not the center, per se, but the influence the center
> ts upon the universal whole. And when the world must integrate nationalism
> universalism, there must take place the destruction of those elements which had
> n root as a result of a constricted nationalism" (Kook 1961: 160, translated in
> r 1995: 261).

ectical character of the relationship between universalism and par-
sm is illustrated by another passage from the same work:

> quality of universalism always fills the hearts of all noble spirits, and they feel
> ed if they are fenced in and circumscribed within their own national circle. But
> people which possesses complete universality in the depths of its soul [...] always
> res (of its members) deeds which clearly engrave the character of this people
> within itself, and which deeds become imbued with a multitude of lofty and
> rsal ideals [...] Restriction in deed and expansion in spirit jointly constitute the
> ary core of the nature of Israel; it is, at one and the same time, "a people that
> dwell alone" and "a light unto the nations" (Kook 1961: 151–152, translated in
> r 1995: 265–266).

adily be seen from this passage that Rabbi Kook does not see the
list and particularist thrusts as being opposed – rather, they are in
each other. The Jewish people would not survive in history without
sms to ensure its survival as a separate people, yet the purpose of
vival is ultimately outer-directed. What Rabbi Kook above refers
nstricted nationalism" can perhaps be understood to mean simply
ession of nationalism which is cut off from this broader goal, and
ereby becomes an end-in-itself. This would, for him, constitute a
the very core teachings and purpose of Jewish spirituality. This
s well as the dialectical tension and reciprocity between universal
cularist concerns are evident in the following passage:

> t souls cannot disassociate themselves from the most universal concerns. All
> esire and aspire for is the universal good [...] But the whole is constituted of
> erless particulars, particular individuals and particular communities [...] Love

such as the first Chief Rabbi of Palestine, Rabbi A
died in 1935. It is thus well worth examining his

For Rabbi Kook, the dichotomy between se
ism is an illusion which arises from our limited
things in parts rather than grasp the totality. Ofte
things fit together and do not grasp the fact that t
as part of a broader matrix. I would argue that t
ing how universalism and particularism fit toge
If we look at things this way, then there can l
Jewish particularism and universalism, because
of each other. Nationalism, and for Rabbi Kook t
tion to its ancestral land, fulfilled a genuinely rec
nation of Israel to recover from the spiritual tin
generations of exile had engendered, and perm
by building a utopian society based on the tea
this is a necessary step, for him, in the unfolc
role in history. His vision melds a particularis
turn to Zion and rebirth of Israel as a nation
version of the redemption of all mankind. Spir
physical, historical process, and Zionism thus
the need to build a society which expresses the
not merely in the ritual realm. Somehow the p
give rise to a deeply universalist, spiritual lon
seems deeply paradoxical, but is not, precisely
nationalism are never ends in themselves but
correctly understood only when seen in the co
delivering through history a message which be
of humanity. Conversely, at least for the Jewisl
and relies upon a whole range of particularist
So we are not speaking of two poles on oppos
rather of two agendas that can and must work
goal.

In Kabbalistic thinking, to which Rabbi K(
hood can be described as Godliness which ha
cut off from its proper matrix and elevated to t
(see Sholem 1991: 56–87). He saw Jewish natic
Jewish people to Zion in this light: when nat

and c
force
transc

"H
ear
ane
ide
to
all
spe
exe
anc
take
Bel

The die
ticulari

"Th
chol
that
requ
deep
uni
prin
shal
Belf

It can r
univers
need of
mechar
that su
to as "c
any exp
which t
denial c
theme,
and par

"Gre
they
num

in its most luminous aspect has its beng beyond the world, in the divine realm, where there are no contradictions, limits and opposition, only bliss and good [...] When worldly love derives from it, it partakes of much in its nature. Even in its descent it does not become miserly or grudging. When it needs to confine itself, it confines love for the sake of love, it sets a boundary around the good for the sake of the good. When these love-possessed people see the world, especially living creatures full of quarrels, hatred, persecutions and conflicts, they yearn with all their being to share in those aspirations that move life toward comprehensiveness and unity, peace and tranquillity. They feel and they know that the nearness of God, for which they yearn, can only lead to joining themselves with *all* and for the sake of *all* [...] they endeavor with all their might to bring all together, to mend and to unite" (Kook 1984: 456–457, translated in Bokser 1978: 226–228).

There is another observation of Rabbi Kook that I'd like to share, and which is of critical importance for those of us engaged in the work of trying to cross boundaries, fight latency/fanatic thinking, and build bridges between religions. It can perhaps best be summed up by quoting the Roman rhetorican Quintus Aurelius Simacus – "It is reasonable that whatever each of us worships is really to be considered one and the same. We gaze up at the same stars, the sky covers us all, the same universe compasses us [...] Not by one avenue only can we arrive at so tremendous a secret."[14] Or as Rabbi Kook put it in many places in his writings, the truth is so vast and so rich, and so multifaceted that it cannot be fully expressed in any one position or theory. As a full-blown metaphysical monist, Rabbi Kook believed that only the One is real, leaving no room for ontological plurality. To quote Prof. Tamar Ross: "Plurality and diversity are merely the function of man's limited perceptions. Nevertheless, the fact that his perceptions are partial manifestations of the One is what gives them their validity. The task of finite minds is to try to try to reconstruct a facsimile of the ultimate unity that is God's." But "reality is so all-encompassing and rich that it can never be contained in an anyone formulation of truth" (Ross 1996: 89+91).

This mode of thinking should not be mistaken for the kind of toleration espoused by modern secular liberalism which arises from unqualified relativism; it is based rather on a deeply religious world view in which even ostensibly "heretical" positions reflect elements of the one truth, and which asserts that by exposing itself to other partial glimpses of truth, each religion or world view can be completed and thereby strengthened, its

---

[14] Letter, written in A.D. 384, to the Christian Emperor Valentinian II, pleading for the continuation of pagan ceremonies. Published in Hooper and Schwartz (1991: ch. 10).

perception being constantly refined by exposure to seemingly conflicting ideas. Indeed, in Rabbi Kook's mystical epistemology, all human truths are but partial, occluded glimpses of a reality that can never be fully comprehended by any one system of beliefs.

Listen to how Kook himself speaks about these issues:

> "Despite differences of opinion among religions and faiths, among races and climes, we should try to comprehend the different groups and peoples of the world to the best of our ability, to learn their nature and their characteristics so that we might know how to build human love [...] And narrow-mindedness, which causes one to see all that is outside the bounds one one's own nation [...] as naught but ugliness and impurity is one of the worst kinds of darkness which completely destroys the whole structure of spiritual good for whose light every noble soul yearns" (Kook 1990: 405, translated in Kaplan and Shatz 1995: 193).

A necessary corollary of this view is the doctrine that all dimensions of reality, including human cultures and religions, are revelations of the divine; therefore, just as the divine is infinite, its manifestation takes on an infinite number of forms and ideas, each of which is nevertheless imbued with holiness and truth according to its own understanding.[15] So although all systems have in them some grain or spark of truth, Rabbi Kook criticized any religious world-view that claimed exclusive access to the truth; it is through the complementarity and even clash of opposing ideas that truth can be glimpsed or clarified. While this perception is not unique in the history of religious mysticism, its significance as an idea that was expressed within the heart of rigorously Orthodox Judaism cannot be overstated, because it allowed Rabbi Kook to reconcile Orthodox theology, which claims that the Jew possessed a revealed truth that no one else had, with a world-view which claims that in fact all religions and all modes of thinking are incomplete and in need of each other. According to Rabbi Kook's model, Judaism has much to teach the world, but it also has much to learn from other religions, as well as non-believers.

How does all this relate to compassion? In reality, our ability to act with empathy and compassion is often limited by our views of the Other. For compassion to be possible, tolerance and respect are first required. But for many believers in Orthodox faiths, tolerance for others is often merely a pragmatic concession, and is thereby half-hearted. Rabbi Kook's view is

---

[15] See Kook (1984: 403): "[...] each and every spark of multiplicity contains within it the blessing of the greatness of the Infinite" (Author's translation).

certainly not a full-blown ideological pluralism. In his view there is certainly such a thing as error and untruth, and these he uncompromisingly rejects. There are ideas that are precious only because of what they might become when enveloped within a larger context. But his multidimensional idea of truth and his perception of the underlying unity of all peoples and the partialness of all truth-claims affords us a workable model for emphasizing the positive role of all faiths, and is thus of critical importance for the task of changing the attitudes which so many believers have towards outsiders.

I am no believer in apologetics. But I think it can fairly be said that in expanding the circle of those to whom we are ethically obligated, and in underscoring so powerfully the universality of Jewish teaching with regard to the holiness of all people, figures like Menachem haMeiri and Rabbi Kook were not so much innovating as leading a revival moment by returning us to the original core message of Judaism which had, perhaps inevitably, been somewhat submerged during the many centuries of exile, persecution, and struggle for mere survival in the midst of hostile cultures.

In Judaism we have no literal, uninterpreted texts, and it is the task of the scholars and teachers in each generation to figure out how to apply fundamental principles such as the ones we have spoken about to real life; when to give more weight to values such as universalism and compassion, and when to subvert them to narrower nationalistic concerns. There are a whole range of psychological and historical issues which bring religious leaders, as well as adherents of every religion, to tend to retreat into narrowness, parochialism, and exclusive self-concern. But there are also many great souls in all camps, who wage unstinting war against everything that narrows and constrains the human spirit.

Within every traditional religious community one detects a tendency to deride as inauthentic any leader who has the courage to think broadly, and to cross boundaries, and who dares to interpret religious texts in a way which doesn't conform to the agenda of extremists. Many people, whether religious or secular, react to anything which challenges their prejudices with fear and rage. Our challenge as religious leaders is to raise a generation of believers who have enough confidence in themselves to allow this narrowness itself to be challenged, and to allow themselves to perceive the truth and holiness that is so abundant in all peoples and in all traditions. In this way we will come to more closely resemble God, "whose compassion is over *all* his creatures" (Psalm 145:9).

References

Banschick, M., 2009: *Religion: Where are the Adults?* (unpublished manuscript).

Belfer, E., 1995: The Land of Israel and Historical Dialectics in the Thought of Rav Kook: Zionism and Messianism, in L. Kaplan and D. Shatz (eds), *Rabbi Abraham Isaac Kook and Jewish Spirituality*, New York.

Birnbaum, P. (ed), 1949: *Daily Prayer Book*, New York.

Bokser, B.Z. (ed), 1978: *Abraham Isaac Kook – The Lights of Penitence, The Moral Principles, Lights of Holiness, Essays, Letters and Poems*, New York.

Buber, M., 1956: The Question to the Single One, in: W. Herberg (ed), *The Writings of Martin Buber*, New York.

Cohen, A. (ed), 1947: *The Soncino Chumash*, London.

Gandhi, M., 1993: *The Story of My Experiments With Truth*, Boston.

Greenberg, I., 1988: *The Jewish Way: Living the Holidays*, New York.

Heschel, A.J., 1969: *The Prophets*, New York.

Hooper, F. and M. Schwartz, 1991: *Roman Letters: History from a Personal Point of View*, Detroit.

Ish-Shalom, B., 1995: Tolerance and Its Theoretical Basis in the Teaching of Rav Kook, in L. Kaplan and D. Shatz, *Rabbi Abraham Isaac Kook and Jewish Spirituality*, New York.

Kook, A.I., 1961: *Lights*, Jerusalem.

—, 1984: *The Lights of Holiness*, Vol. II, Jerusalem.

—, 1990: *The Lights of Holiness*, Vol. IV, Jerusalem.

Marty, M.E. and R.S. Appleby, 1994: *Fundamentalisms Observed*, Chicago.

Ross, T., 1996: Between Metaphysical and Liberal Pluralism, *Academy for Jewish Studies Review* 21/1.

Scholem, G., 1991: *On the Mystical Shape of the Godhead*, New York.

Simon, E., 1975: The Neighbor (Re'a) Whom We Shall Love, in: M. Fox (ed), *Modern Jewish Ethics: Theory and Practice*, Columbus.

Soloveitchik, J.B., 1983: *Halakhic Man*, Philadelphia.

Temkin, S.D., 1974: *The New World of Reform*, Bridgeport.

6. Chapter

Compassion – The Teachings of R. Nachman of Breslav

ALON GOSHEN-GOTTSTEIN

RABBI NACHMAN OF BRESLAV, a late 18th – early 19th century hassidic master, is an original thinker, whose thought is both a continuation of longstanding spiritual traditions and an expression of his own personal spiritual experiences and the specific intuitions and understandings that arose from it. His unique literary style and associative way of thinking are best understood as a way of giving expression to his direct spiritual cognitions, clothing and expressing them in the language of classical Jewish homiletics.[1] In reading R. Nachman, then, we are dealing with original spiritual intuitions, born within the matrix of and expressed in continuity with broader Jewish notions. The power of the spiritual life of R. Nachman and the fact that so much of his writing is born of personal experience and original intuition makes him a fascinating and inspiring figure to study, on any topic. My personal love for him and the inspiration I continually draw from his writings lead me to approach his work as a resource for tackling issues upon which I seek to reflect. Compassion is a theme that comes up in several contexts in R. Nachman's work and it is fair to characterize it as an important element in his thinking, and implicitly in his personal religious experience. How R. Nachman works through

---

[1] For a biography of R. Nachman, see Arthur Green, *Tormented Master: A Life of Rabbi Nahman of Bratslav,* University, Ala., University of Alabama Press, 1979. I assume most readers of this essay will not be able to handle scholarly literature in Hebrew and will therefore not reference it. For a bibliography of works on R. Nachman and his movement, Breslav hassidism, see David Assaf, *Breslav - An Annotated Bibliography,* Jerusalem, Zalman Schazar Center, 2000 [Hebrew].

the notion of compassion, its applications and the range of ideas he associates with it is quite unique, and on the whole not part of a broader thematization of compassion in Jewish literature. The present project that seeks to bring together insights on compassion, drawn from various religious traditions, will benefit from following R. Nachman's train of thought. I therefore permit myself to focus this presentation on his thought, rather than attempting a more conventional portrait of how compassion is conceptualized in Jewish thought, as a whole.[2]

Rather than attempt a synthetic presentation of compassion in R. Nachman's thought,[3] I would like to present several key teachings of R. Nachman, each of which thematizes compassion differently, in relation to other core values. How we understand any cardinal value is not only a matter of what we may have to say about it but also of how it intersects with other ideas and values and the range of associations that are brought to bear on that value. In what follows, I will present a range of associations that R. Nachman brings to bear on compassion, thereby stretching our thinking on the subject. The thicker the web of associations, the more central an idea may be said to be within the broader economy of a system of thought. In what follows I hope to demonstrate indirectly the centrality of compassion to R. Nachman's thought through the associative web within which compassion is weaved.

I. Compassion - The Ground of Being, the Purpose of Creation

One of R. Nachman's most famous teachings, Teaching 64, discusses creation and how to cope with the fundamental existential questions, some of

---

[2] For a concise recent statement, see the article "Compassion in Judaism", in *Encyclopedia of Love in World Religions*, ed. Yudit Kornberg Greenberg, Santa Barbara, ABC-CLIO, 2008, vol. 1, pp. 132-133. Actually, very little has been written on the topic, and there is no monograph length treatment of compassion in Jewish thought.

[3] I have attempted that in "Judaism: the Battle for Survival, the struggle for Compassion", in *Religion, Society and the Other: Hostility, Hospitality and the Hope of Human Flourishing*, ed. Alon Goshen-Gottstein, forthcoming, Fordham University Press.

which are beyond the comprehension of the human mind, associated with it.[4] This celebrated teaching opens with the following statement:

> God created the world because of His compassion, because He wanted to reveal His compassion, and if the world had not been created, who would He show his compassion to? Therefore He created all of creation, from the beginning of the emanation to the final center point of the physical world, in order to show His compassion.

The question of why God created the world is a crux of all religious thought, including Jewish thought. While the question that opens the discussion is standard, R. Nachman's answer is not. As far as I am aware, he is the first person to frame the answer in terms of compassion. Compassion is the *telos* of creation and the act of creation is grounded and motivated in divine compassion. Compassion requires the duality of creator and creation. God's compassion is such a fundamental dimension of His being, that it requires an arena within which it can be manifested and that arena is creation itself.

Compassion is not simply the ultimate purpose of creation, it is also what governs all aspects of creation, manifesting itself in every distinct stage of the process. Moreover, compassion is not limited to the higher rungs of the order of creation, where it is recognizable. It extends down to the most physical level whose creation may be construed as an act of compassion and which provides the opportunity and possibility for manifesting further divine compassion. All that was created is necessary for the manifestation of divine compassion.

The meaning of this statement is that all that God does within the field of creation is an expression of his goodness and compassion. R. Nachman specifies that this overarching *raison d'être* of creation, addresses creation down to its most physical and most detailed aspects. This means that nothing in creation is excluded from Divine compassion and goodness. This statement is of great significance, in light of the themes which R. Nachman will discuss farther along in this teaching. In what follows, R. Nachman discusses the epistemological limitations placed upon our consciousness by the very structure of creation. These limitations touch upon our ability to deal adequately and correctly with questions of theodicy. It is important,

---

[4] On this teaching, see my Speech, Silence, Song : Epistemology and Theodicy in a Teaching of R. Nahman of Breslav, *Philosophia* 30,1-4, 2003, pp. 143-187. I did not consider seriously enough how compassion is thematized in this teaching in that article, though such consideration would not alter my presentation.

therefore, that prior to any statement that places a limitation upon the human capacity to know, R. Nachman makes a positive statement, affirming the compassion that finds expression in all aspects of creation. This meta-statement expresses the ultimate religious perspective, which the subject-matter of this teaching threatens, and which is ultimately reaffirmed by R. Nachman.

If compassion is the goal and logic of creation, this may be taken a step further, suggesting that in fact all of life and all of being takes place within the context of compassion. Compassion may thus be considered not only the purpose, but the very substance of life and creation. This emerges later on the teaching, when R. Nachman revisits the opening statement, in light of the kabbalisitc doctrine of *zimzum*, divine contraction, an important theme within this teaching. Towards the end of the teaching, R. Nachman states:

> The principle of creation was for the sake of His compassion ... For in everything that was created within the empty space (i.e. the space of the *zimzum*, cleared by God in order to make room for creation) there is contraction of His compassion, and He created this specific thing in the particular form and image it has, in accordance with His compassion, for His compassion, blessed be He, necessitated that this matter will be so. Because compassion is the root of all creation, for everything was created in order to manifest His compassion.

One would have expected divine Wisdom to be the reason for why the various details of creation have come into being, while divine compassion might be the overarching cause for the act of creation. However, R. Nachman associates all stages of creation with compassion. Compassion dictates how creation is to unfold. In other words, everything within creation, every detail within it, may be considered an occasion for manifesting divine compassion and a way of serving that goal. God has given thought to how construct every fine detail within creation, so as to maximize its impact as a means of manifesting His compassion. R. Nachman is more radical still. R. Nachman speaks of the *zimzum*, the contraction of divine being and light in order to make room for creation, as the contraction of divine compassion. If it is divine compassion that has to be contracted in order to make room for the world, this suggests that compassion is the very nature of divine being. Compassion is thus a legitimate way of referring to the divine being, alongside more conventional ways of referring to God's being, as well as the *zimzum*, in terms of light or being.[5] Now, if it divine compassion that is being contracted, this suggests compassion is much more than simply the purpose of creation. It is the very ground of being. It is the divine itself. God is compassion. Therefore, every act in creation, whether it is an act of self limitation or the giving of form to life within the structures of creation, is an expression of this divine compassion. Differently put: compassion is the substance of life. It is not simply a human quality, a virtue. It is the essence, or at least one way of talking, of the divine. That creation takes place within compassion and that compassion informs decisions regarding the particulars of creation allows us to consider creation as in some way divine. Creation with and within compassion is creation within God.

This conceptualization challenges us to think in fresh ways about creation, both the act and its outcome. It changes our valuation of creation, highlighting all that is good in it and featuring compassion as the means of expressing the fundamental goodness of creation. Being created means being a recipient of God's compassion. We are created through an act of compassion and our very creatureliness calls for divine compassion. Compassion thus emerges as the most fundamental attitude to life.

Now, R. Nachman has only spoken of divine compassion. His way of conceptualizing and presenting classical kabbalistic notions of *zimzum* serves the epistemological challenges of dealing with theodicy and other limitations of human understanding, as expounded in Teaching 64. R. Nachman makes no attempt to develop the moral implications of grounding creation in divine compassion. But such reflections naturally emerge from thoughtful consideration of the move he has made. If creation is grounded in compassion, this has moral consequences for us and must condition our behavior as well. Compassion emerges as the fundamental characteristic of creation, thereby inviting us to act in accordance with this ground and ground rule of all being. If God has created out of compassion, surely we too must treat all of creation in similar light. And compassion is neither limited to our co-religionists nor to our brothers and sisters in the human

---

[5] In the opening of Teaching 64, R. Nachman refers to the divine contraction in terms of light. The same is true for the opening of Teaching 49. In this R. Nachman is faithful to the language of R. Isaac Luria, from whom he takes the notion of *zimzum*. R. Nachman's original thinking is expressed by substituting compassion for light.

species. Compassion as the ground of creation invites us to practice compassion towards all life, all creation. Taking this a step further, we note again that compassion is what accounts for the particularity of every detail in creation. If details of creation are governed by compassion, it would seem that compassion should inform not only our broadest intentions, but also the specifics of our actions. Thinking how our actions might increase compassion is not simply an act of *imitatio dei.* It is a way of attuning ourselves to the very fabric of being, informed by the ultimate divine purpose and the careful attention it has given to every detail of creation. Compassion thus emerges as a means of being in harmony with the world, as well as of attuning oneself to the purposes of the creator. I cannot think of a more profound way of grounding compassion. Compassion is not simply an excellent moral virtue nor is it limited to human relations. It is a basic, perhaps the most basic, law of life, inviting us to a way of living that accords with the deeper cosmic purpose.

Compassion's cosmic status would best account for the following novel statement, R. Nachman makes in another teaching: The world[6] needs great compassion, both spiritually and physically. And every one asks for compassion,[7] and does not know where it is. And compassion is present before everyone's eyes, [8] as it says "it is not far, and not in heaven".[9]

Compassion is the fundamental human quest. It is required to address both spiritual and physical needs, seeking divine compassion and mercy. Our condition is one of ignorance, as we seek divine compassion and struggle to locate and identify it. However, such struggle is really born of ignorance, for compassion is here and now, ever present. R. Nachman paraphrases a verse in Deut. 30, 11-12, in order to prove that compassion is not far and distant, but close by and readily available. In light of Teaching 64, we may well account for why compassion is omnipresent. If compassion is the stuff of creation, then it is indeed not in heaven and not far off. It is

---

[6] Following colloquial usage, this is a way of saying "people", rather than the cosmos, even though R. Nachman's thought could justify also a broader application of the term.

[7] R. Nachman uses in this teaching the form *rachamim*, rather than *rachmanut*, as in Teaching 64. This could also be translated as mercy.

[8] This comes close to suggesting that compassion is omnipresent, and perhaps might even be thus translated. Hebrew does not have one word to designate the notion of omnipresence.

[9] Teaching 105.

what informs every act of creation and what provides the deeper logic and purpose for every detail of creation. It is thus present in the very fabric of creation, available as creation's most basic substance.[10] We are, however, in ignorance of it, an ignorance that may be traced back to the original *zimzum*, wherein God contracts his light and his compassion, thereby obscuring it from our understanding.[11] We thus search for what we have before our eyes, seeking to find the hidden ground of Being, which is hidden from us only by our own ignorance. This leads to the second theme to be presently explored, the relationship between knowledge, ignorance, and compassion. One final point, however, before moving on.

Deut. 30,11, that R. Nachman just quoted, speaks of the commandment that God commands us today, without specifying what it is, as not being far and distant. Did R. Nachman understand this unspecified commandment as a reference to compassion? Is his application of Deut. 30,11 limited to the potential linguistic expression of omnipresence or immanence, or does it go further, amounting to a complete reading of the verse and the commandment of which it speaks? If the latter is the case, then R. Nachman has also identified a scriptural basis for compassion, and perhaps even for its grounding in creation, in the here and now of the details of creation, not just the above and beyond. If I have not over read R. Nachman, then perhaps we also have here a proof text that grounds human obligation to practice compassion in the existential ground of compassion, that informs all of creation. The commandment to practice omnipresent compassion would ultimately be grounded in the fact that creation itself is the supreme expression of divine compassion.

II. Compassion and Consciousness

Teaching 64 suggests a relationship between metaphysics and epistemology. *Zimzum* effects not only Being itself, but also our ability to know and understand. The connection between compassion and consciousness is one of the major motifs in R. Nachman's reflections on compassion. The mes-

---

[10]　See further *Likutey Moharan* 2,49: "God is full of compassion, and the entire world is full of compassion".

[11]　We have already noted that R. Nachman casts the *zimzum* in epistemological terms. The hiding of divine compassion from human recognition and understanding is thus perfectly in accordance with how these ideas are presented in his teachings.

sage is quite simple: compassion is grounded in consciousness. The Hebrew term is *da'at*, which can be rendered as mind, understanding, and in my view is best captured as consciousness. The idea is that compassion is not simply a quality we have or possess. Rather, it is something that grows in us and its growth is related to the evolution of consciousness. As our mind and understanding expand, so does our capacity to have compassion. Someone with a limited view of reality and with limited horizons of consciousness will be self involved and unable to extend compassion to his or her environs. Broadening the horizons of awareness is in fact growing into the broader divine awareness and therefore a gateway into participating in divine compassion. The association of compassion and *da'at* suggests that compassion is not simply an emotion, or a feeling towards another. It is, rather, the flow of being and goodwill towards another, that is grounded in a higher spiritual realization, born of the expanded consciousness, *da'at*, and the broader understanding of the meaning of life that it brings with it. While it touches our hearts, it is more than emotion. It is the expression in the emotional, perhaps also in the volitional realm, of a movement that is born of recognition of fundamental spiritual realities. Because we perceive spiritual reality and partake of the divine vision of life, creation and their ultimate purpose, we share in divine compassion. Divine compassion may accordingly be presented as the drive that impels our spiritual evolution forward and that shows care for our overall wellbeing, along with the wellbeing of all of creation. In fact, if compassion is another way of referring to God's very being, then what *da'at* provides is the capacity to comprehend the true nature of Being, creation grounded in the divine Being. From such fuller comprehension arises the identification with divine compassion and its extension to all beings.

The association of compassion and consciousness is repeated in various teachings of R. Nachman. Let us look at several of them.

> When a person is in need of compassion, God sends him compassion, that he may extend it to others, and thereby compassion is extended to him, as our sages have taught, "whoever has compassion on others, himself receives compassion thereby" (Talmud Shabbat 151b) … And compassion is dependent upon *da'at* (consciousness). Whoever has awareness has compassion. Because anger, which is the opposite of compassion, is due to ignorance … Now, a sick person himself requires compassion. But he must have compassion upon others and that is a function of consciousness. And Shabbat is an expression of consciousness … And on Shabbat awareness is extended to everyone. This is why one says to the sick person, whom one visits on the

Shabbat, "it (meaning the Shabbat) can have compassion", meaning that the Shabbat, which is an aspect of consciousness, can make you have compassion upon others ... And if you have compassion, then surely compassion will be extended from Heaven towards you.[12]

This teaching pulls together several principles. The first is that compassion is a kind of existential circle. It flows from one to another, with the extension of compassion as the gateway to its reception. Thus, if one requires compassion, one must join the existential cycle of compassion, by extending it to others, thereby entering the cycle of giving and receiving. This cycle may originate in Heaven, but it unites the human and divine spheres in one act of continuous giving. As we give below, so we receive from above. A second theme is that compassion is grounded in consciousness. Here R. Nachman actually offers a way of accessing divine consciousness. The way is Shabbat. Shabbat is not simply a day of rest but a spiritual reality, whose foundation is the entering into divine presence and divine compassion. A higher state of consciousness is available on Shabbat. Entry into this state of consciousness makes it possible for the sick person to extend compassion to others, thereby making him a worthy recipient of divine compassion. We also note how anger and compassion are contrasted with each other. Anger seems to be basic to human psychology. In several places R. Nachman seems to suggest that anger is a component of human psychology that requires transformation.[13] Human spiritual evolution may be measured in terms of our ability to transform anger into compassion. The ongoing struggle against the anger in our hearts cannot be attained simply through will power and self control. Rather, it requires the elevation to a higher state of consciousness that provides the means of transformation for innate anger. Consciousness is thus the means of transformation of anger into compassion.

The relationship between compassion and consciousness and understanding can be conceived in various ways. Probably the most common is the recognition that consciousness is the ground of compassion.[14] In some contexts *da'at* is the condition not only for extending compassion, but also for receiving compassion. The point is not that one who lacks *da'at* should not receive compassion. On the contrary, R. Nachman is explicit about

---

[12] *Likutey Moharan* 119.
[13] See, for example, *Likutey Moharan* 18.
[14] In addition to the sources already discussed, see also *Likutey Moharan* 105 and 56.

the fact that there is nothing more deserving of compassion than the lack of *da'at*.[15] Rather, due to the close association of *da'at* and compassion, one lacking in *da'at* may be cruel. To such a person compassion should not be extended, as it might reinforce the cruel behavior or nature. However, withholding compassion is itself an expression of compassion, as it amounts to providing for those who cannot receive compassion the very food they require. Compassion is thus universal, though its application may differ radically, depending on the recipient.[16]

The recognition that consciousness is the ground for compassion allows R. Nachman to revisit biblical eschatological prophecies. Compassion's ground in consciousness is not only a spiritual and existential principle, but is also the focus of a vision of history and provides the rationale for how history can change in the future. Prophecies describing change in human nature and in nature in general can be understood as the outcome of growth in consciousness, which would bring about fundamental changes in human behavior.

> Compassion depends on *da'at,* as it says (Isa. 11): "No harm nor destruction shall be wrought throughout all my holy mountain; for the land will have become full of the knowledge of God, as the waters cover the sea". For in the future *da'at* will greatly increase, and then there will be no harm or cruelty, because compassion will spread about, through *da'at*, since compassion depends upon *da'at*. [17]

The basic insight captured in all these teachings is that through consciousness, the higher spiritual understanding, we gain compassion. A higher vision allows us to have compassion within a given situation. Such compassion provides a drive for change and motivates one to act. Thus, com-

---

[15] See *Likutey Moharan* 106.

[16] See *Likutey Moharan* 2,7,1 and compare 2,8,2.

[17] *Likutey Moharan* 2,8,2. For a grounding of eschatological visions in the increase of the knowledge of God, see Maimonides, Laws of Kings 12,5. Maimonides cites the latter part of the verse in Isaiah, after describing the future age as an age without wars. From Maimonides it would seem that there will be no wars because of the abundance of goods, making war superfluous. People would accordingly devote themselves to the knowledge of God. Knowledge of God does not seem to be the cause of the future peaceful world, but rather its outcome. The plain sense of the verse in Isaiah does suggest a causality, according to which knowledge is the ground of future peace. R. Nachman's reading, and the place he allots for compassion, allow the plain sense of the verse to resonate powerfully. In light of this reading, the collocation of compassion and peace, found in *Likutey Moharan* 56,6 makes particularly good sense.

passion for lack of knowledge translates itself into action that would fill
the lack.

> Poverty is [poverty] from knowledge (Talmud Nedarim 41). And for this (i.e., lack
> of knowledge) one ought to have compassion, for there is nothing more deserving of
> compassion. And such poverty applies in general and in relation to oneself. In general,
> regarding a person who lacks understanding[18] in the service of God, someone who
> possesses understanding should share it with him. And in relation to oneself, there
> are times when one lacks consciousness, and this state is called small mindedness,
> and one should fortify oneself to come to great mindedness.[19]

Compassion to the poor is to fill the poor's need, be it the other or oneself.
Compassion thus drives to action. In other cases, the practice of compassion calls for withholding of actual kindness, for fear of growing the evil
in others, as noted above.

In one working out of the relations of compassion and consciousness,
R. Nachman makes us aware of an important paradox and how it may be
resolved.

> Compassion is in the aspect of the acronym ISRAEL found in the Hebrew verse, and
> the Lord Shaday will give you compassion (Gen. 43,14). That is, that God will give
> us the compassion, He will entrust it in our hands. Because from God's perspective,
> it may be that even great illness and all forms of suffering are expressions of His
> compassion. For surely all that God does to a person, even great sufferings, all is pure
> compassion. But we ask that God should give and entrust compassion into our hands.
> Because we do not understand His compassion and we are also unable to receive that
> compassion of His. Therefore we ask that God should entrust compassion into our
> hands, that we ourselves should have compassion upon ourselves, and when it comes
> to us, compassion is manifested in the plain sense, to be healed from sickness, and
> the likes.[20]

To talk of consciousness begs the question of what level of consciousness
we are talking about. The drive for raising consciousness is one of moving
from lesser to greater awareness, from human to divine understanding.
But reaching a divine understanding is potentially counter productive to
the application of compassion. After all, as we have already seen, God is
Himself compassion. How can one request anything from God - how can

---

[18] The Hebrew *sekhel* can be translated as understanding, knowledge or consciousness.
While I think the latter captures the intention most fully, the first translation reads most
easily in English.

[19] *Likutey Moharan* 106.

[20] *Likutey Moharan* 2,62.

one request God's compassion - when in fact anything that God does, suffering included, is already founded upon divine compassion? Taking seriously compassion as the ground of being and the profound motivation for all divine action would actually lead to inaction. Compassion could be configured as simply rising to the heights of divine consciousness, understanding the cause of suffering and how it too is grounded in divine compassion. Much like the inaction we practice towards the evil, we might be tempted to become resigned to such treatment by God, recognizing the ubiquity of compassion in the fabric of creation and in the profundity of the divine will. This would make prayer superfluous, perhaps impossible. Recognizing the depth of compassion would disable its active practice, making it an exercise in raising consciousness, rather than in extending relief and help to the world.[21] The answer to this conundrum is the limitation of consciousness. Perhaps this echoes the initial limitation of the *zimzum,* itself founded upon compassion, as we noted above. However, R. Nachman does not appeal to the term here. He merely constructs compassion in human terms, rather than in relation to God's own understanding. Accordingly, we beseech God to entrust compassion to us, so that compassion will accord with the human understanding of what is considered compassionate, rather than with the potential higher divine understanding of compassion, that could sustain suffering within it. The plain sense of compassion, based in human understanding, is thus upheld, at the expense of the higher consciousness of God. Here we encounter an opposite movement to that encountered in most texts. Whereas the usual movement is one in which compassion is born of consciousness, and therefore the greater the consciousness the greater the compassion, here consciousness is limited to the human understanding. Configuring compassion in relation to consciousness in this way provides a theoretical basis for extending compassion into acts of kindness. Perhaps even more importantly, it provides a foundation for prayer.[22]

---

[21] How powerfully compassion is a drive for effecting change in the world through prayer may be seen from *Likutey Moharan* 2,105.

[22] In aramaic prayer is called "compassion", a fact noted by R. Nachman. We have here one more indication for the centrality of prayer in his spiritual experience. The most central spiritual practice grounds and provides an approach to the fundamental nature of the divine - compassion.

III. Compassion and Leadership

Perhaps the most powerful indication of the active nature of compassion is to be found in how R. Nachman relates compassion to leadership. Given the strong mystical and experiential background of R. Nachman's writing, many readers assume that R. Nachman's teachings are always in some way autobiographical, even when R. Nachman is not speaking in the first person. If so, the association of compassion and leadership would be not only a matter of theory and reflection on compassion and its application, but a testimony to the power that drove his own leadership of the community. The following words, describing the archetypal Jewish leader, Moses, may provide a window unto R. Nachman's own understanding of the purpose and goal of his leadership.

1. "For the compassionate one will be their leader" (Isa.49) - this suggests that only someone possessing compassion can be a leader ...

2. And such a compassionate one is found only in Moses our teacher, who was the leader of Israel and is its future leader ... For Moses our teacher had true compassion for Israel, and was willing to give his life for Israel, casting aside his own soul, having no concern for himself whatsoever. [We know this] because God offered to make of him a great nation (Ex. 32) [following the sin of the golden calf, thereby replacing Israel with Moses' progeny], but he paid no attention to this offer at all, and said in response only: " Forgive their sin and if not, erase me from the book you have written". For he was compassionate and a true leader. And he engaged in making the world civilized, that the world should be settled by human beings. Because the most important thing about a human being is *da'at*. And whoever lacks *da'at* is not civilized and can't be called a human being properly, but only a human shaped animal. And Moses our teacher had compassion, and he engaged in making the world civilized, that the world should be settled and filled with human beings, that is possessors of knowledge, for he opened for us the light of *da'at*, as it says: "you have been given the understanding that the Lord is God" (Deut. 4). For Moses opened for us the *da'at*, and revealed to us that there is a God, who rules the earth.

3. Because the core of compassion is when Israel, the holy nation, fall, God forbid, into sin. For this is the greatest compassion of all compassions. Because all the sufferings in the world do not count at all compared with the heavy burden of sins, God forbid. For when Israel fall into sin, God forbid, this is a very heavy burden, that is unbearable ... And this is the core of compassion, to have compassion upon Israel, the holy nation, to take them out of the heavy burden of sins. And this is why Moses our teacher, whenever Israel fell into any sin, would give his soul for them, and pray for them.[23]

---

[23] *Likutey Moharan* 2,7,1-3.

Compassion is, once again, understood in terms of *da'at*. Endowing human beings with *da'at* is the supreme act of compassion. Compassion and wisdom thus figure time and again in close association. Because Moses possesses God's knowledge fully, he has the true perspective on reality. This perspective allows him to know God, as well as the soul and the meaning of what it is to be a human being. Compassion leads to populating the world and making it civilized, by spreading the knowledge of God. From the language used by R. Nachman it seems that the burden of sins, referred to in relation to Israel, is even more weighty than the general human condition of ignorance. It is this pain that impels Moses to offer his life, in a sacrificial movement, in order to remove the burden of sins from Israel. Exodus 32, 32's reference to the book God has written, a rare moment of self referentiality in the Bible, is read back into reality and understood as Moses' offer to give his life for Israel. The strategy succeeds and Israel are forgiven, based on this offer of self sacrifice. Compassion leads to the highest form of sacrifice- self sacrifice.

Leadership is a completely spiritual affair. Even though Moses also functions as a political leader, as the Rabbis understood, as well as a military leader, these dimensions of leadership are ignored. Instead, the leader is the teacher, the one who removes ignorance and makes God's knowledge known, the one who lifts up the burden of sin and suffering. This description of leadership and its scope fits well with the range of activities in which R. Nachman himself engaged. While the description of Moses' offer of his life is traditional, his description of the painful burden of sin is not. It is reasonable to suggest that here we hear R. Nachman's own voice, as it offers us a window into his own compassion-driven exercise of leadership.

Leadership is not something to be sought out or desired. The honor and status that are associated with leadership provide motivation that is the opposite of the ideal compassion-based motivation. In fact, a true spiritual leader will refuse leadership. Again, Moses provides the example, with his refusal of leadership, as recounted in Exodus, chapter 3.[24]

R. Nachman tells us that the true spiritual master has practiced the sweetening of anger. Wherever anger arose, he would appease it with compassion, allowing compassion to subdue and sweeten the anger. R. Nach-

---

[24] For the present and following section, see *Likutey Moharan* 18,2.

man uses a very particular expression in this context. The Zaddikim, spiritual masters, are crowned with compassion. Their practice of sweetening anger with compassion makes them a crown of compassion. R. Nachman may be alluding to the understanding that the force of compassion resides in the spiritual center known in the Kabbalah as the crown, located at the top of the head. The high value attached to compassion may be based on the recognition that compassion has its source in the highest spiritual center. This could also account for the idea we saw at the beginning of our study, according to which the world was created due to God's compassion. The crown is associated with will and higher purpose, and is the source of the creative process. If creation draws from the crown and the crown is associated with compassion, compassion readily emerges as the underlying drive behind creation.

Reference to compassion in terms of the crown also allows R. Nachman to shift from the crown of compassion to the crown of leadership. A condition for undertaking communal leadership is that the leader is already crowned. Only one who is already crowned with compassion should accept the responsibility of leadership.

IV. Conclusion – Applying R. Nachman's Wisdom

By way of conclusion, I would like to draw the lessons that R. Nachman's teachings hold for those who contemplate what compassion might mean for us today. The association of compassion and leadership that we have just explored should not mislead us to thinking that compassion is the domain of the choice few, the spiritual masters. While these have mastered compassion, compassion actually belongs to all. Let us recall that the spiritual masters practice the sweetening of anger with compassion. This suggests an ongoing active effort at cultivating compassion and eradicating anger. This reveals a spiritual practice that is applicable to all and that is universal in scope. While one may not yet attain the fullness of compassion, one may strive and practice towards this goal.

Beyond the possibility for common practice, there is deeper commonality that makes compassion relevant to and within reach of all. Compassion is structured in the very fabric of creation. Such an understanding constitutes a call to uncover that which is foundational. If God creates the world in and through compassion, we have the possibility of uncovering and bringing to light the fundamental spiritual principle that informs all of creation.

However, unlike the practice of compassion, the uncovering of true compassion, grounded in life and creation, is less accessible. The challenge is precisely that the true nature of reality is hidden. Unlike the Hindu tradition that allocates a prominent role in its metaphysical system to ignorance, and even assigns it a special term, *avidya*, the Jewish tradition has not elevated ignorance to such a high level in its systematic reflection. Nevertheless, the emphasis on *da'at*, knowledge and consciousness, leads us to the recognition that it is the lack of *da'at*, ignorance, that accounts for lack of compassion. Compassion cannot be realized simply by goodwill and intention. It requires a deeper knowledge that goes to the root of creation, its purpose and the ultimate goal of all - the knowledge of God. For compassion to be realized, the fullness of knowledge and the fullness of faith are needed.[25] This is a process and as all processes, it requires time. Some master it more fully than others, but all are called to realize it.

R. Nachman offers us a realistic view of compassion. Its spiritual reality eludes as, even as its practice is constant. It may be attained, but only in conjunction with the attainment of wisdom and faith. It is thus the most ubiquitous spiritual reality, but also the most hidden. Realizing compassion is thus a process, a lifelong process. All this is well summarized in the quote we saw above, which serves us well as a conclusion to this essay:

> Every one asks for compassion, and does not know where it is. And compassion is present before everyone's eyes, as it says "it is not far, and not in heaven".[26]

---

[25] On faith as a condition for true compassion, see *Likutey Moharan* 18,2.
[26] *Likutey Moharan* 105.

7. Chapter

Compassion as a Core-Element of Christian Ethics

REINHOLD BERNHARDT

THE GOSPEL OF LUKE relates the famous and wide-spread parable of the Good Samaritan (Luke 10:25–37). Jesus had been asked by an expert in the Jewish Law: "Teacher, what must I do to inherit eternal life?" Jesus replied by asking: "How do you read the Law?" The man answered: "'Love the Lord your God with all your heart and with all your soul and with all your strength and with all your mind'; and, 'Love your neighbour as yourself.'" – "You have answered correctly," Jesus replied. "Do this and you will live." But the man wanted to justify himself, so he asked Jesus, "And who is my neighbour?" In reply Jesus told the following parable: "A man was going down from Jerusalem to Jericho when he fell into the hands of robbers. They stripped him of his clothes, beat him and went away, leaving him half dead with no clothes. A priest happened to be going down the same road, and when he saw the man, passed by on the other side. So too, a Levite, coming to the place and seeing him, passed by on the other side. But as a Samaritan came down the same road and seeing him, he had *compassion* on him. He went to him and bandaged his wounds, pouring on oil and wine. Then he put the man on his own donkey, took him to an inn and cared for him. The next day he took out two silver coins and gave them to the innkeeper. 'Look after him,' he said, 'and when I return, I will reimburse you for any extra expense you may have.' – "Which of these three do you think was a neighbour to the man who fell into the hands of robbers?" The expert in the law replied: "The one who had mercy on him."

In the first section of my paper I would like to employ this parable of the Good Samaritan in order to point up the importance of compassion for the

Christian tradition but also in order to discuss compassion's limitations as
a foundation for Christian ethics. The aim will be to work out a viable and
adequate understanding of compassion. In the second part I will inquire
into the role which compassion can play in interreligious encounters.

I. Compassion as emotion, consciousness and ethical norm

According to the English translation of the parable, the Samaritan felt
"compassion" when he saw the victim of the assault. In the original Greek
text a much stronger expression is used: *splagchnizomai,* meaning that "the
bowels" – as the most interior, most intimate part of the human being –
"turn over", as it were. Nowadays we would prefer to speak of the heart
as the centre of human emotions, but according to the New Testament understanding, the entrails are the location of the emotions. Compassion is
experienced as an interior *revolt* within the emotional condition of one
who is affected by the suffering (Latin: *passio*) of another human being
or of an animal – the suffering, that is to say, of a sentient being, a being
with a soul (Latin: "anima"), and thus able to feel pain. Compassion means
to *share* that suffering, to participate in it, to make it one's own feeling,
to suffer with the sufferer (Latin: *com-passio*). The suffering of the Other
evokes a resonance in me: a co-suffering.

The same expression, "the turning over of the bowels", is used in a
number of other important biblical testimonies. Jesus felt that kind of interior revolt when he saw a crowd of hungry people (Mark 8:2; 6:34, see
also Matt 9:36), when he met two blind men (Matt 20:34) and a leper (Mark
1:41) and when he encountered a mother grieving over her dead son (Luke
7:13). Moreover there are two parables in the New Testament where the
expression is applied even to God himself. One of them is the parable of
the Unmerciful Servant (Matt 18:27); the other is the well-known story of
the Prodigal Son: When he returned to his father – poor, hungry, and dirty
– the father felt a rumbling in his entrails (Luke 15:20). This is to say that
God himself feels compassion for the needy, the poor and oppressed. It is
that which constitutes the most profound basis for a Christian ethics of
solidarity.

But is it sufficient to base ethics on emotions? Isn't that a shaky ground
– highly individualistic and capricious? Compassion would then tend to be
evoked primarily by suffering which occurs close to me or which strikes

people to whom I feel related in one way or the other. The citizens of the U.S.A. were obviously affected more deeply by the victims of Hurricane Katrina in New Orleans than by the victims of the Tsunami in Southeast Asia. Suffering which I experience directly and immediately calls forth a stronger feeling of compassion than suffering which is reported to me by the mass media. Compassion as an emotion can thus be "prejudiced", giving preference to those who suffer at close range to me or who belong to my family or my tribe or my community or my nation or my religion.

In the parable of the Good Samaritan Jesus avoids that preference for the proximal Other and universalizes the commitment to care for the needy whoever and wherever he or she is. Interpreted from the standpoint of the Samaritan it teaches that *everybody* who is in need has to be regarded as one's neighbour[1], because he or she is creature of God and is thus to be respected as *God's* neighbour. Interpreted from the standpoint of the sufferer it teaches that *everybody* who comes to the aid of someone in need has to be regarded as neighbour because he or she acts in the name of God – as *God's* neighbour. The term "neighbourly-love" can thus be understood as referring to a *genitivus objectivus* (the person in need of loving care is the neighbour) or to a *genitivus subjectivus* (the person offering love is the neighbour). In both cases "neighbourhood", according to the Christian understanding, is constituted in the relationship with God, and not by an affection or a relationship between the person in need and the person who cares about him or her. Thus the parable elaborates "neighbourhood" neither in the spatial terms of living together in a social community, nor in the ethnic, cultural or religious terms of belonging to the same people, culture or religion, nor in terms of common interests such as a shared preference for the same soccer-team or employment in the same company or membership in the same political party. "Neighbourhood" is constituted in and through God's salvific will for all his creatures which is at work as a promise and an obligation to care for the needs of persons whom I come to meet, be it personally or as mediated by information. Because I am a creature loved by God, I am empowered to love my neighbour.

As a mere spontaneous and immediate emotion, compassion is indeed insufficient as a basis for Christian ethics. In the context of an ethos of neighbourly love compassion is awareness, an attentiveness which is part

---

[1] For an analysis of the biblical notion of the Other see Evers (2007: 203–207).

of a permanent (habitual) ethical attitude – in traditional terms: the virtue
of charity. "Compassion is not a simple feeling-state but a complex emotional attitude toward another, characteristically involving imaginative
dwelling on the condition of the other person, an active regard for his
good, a view of him as a fellow human being, and emotional responses
of a certain degree of intensity" (Blum 1980: 175).

To approach compassion as an ethical attitude of neighbourly love –
as is characteristic for Christian ethics – does not mean to neglect the importance of the affectional dimension. The *attitude* of compassion becomes
both activated and energized by the *affection* of compassion.[2] On the other
hand, spontaneous emotional energy needs to be channelled into and integrated within the framework of an ethical attitude, where it can become an
integral part of a specific pattern of life-orientation. Compassion thus has
both an emotional and a rational component. While the ethical attitude is
always anchored in a specific religious and cultural tradition, compassion
as affection can be regarded as a universal anthropological capacity able to
transgress the boundaries between ethnic groups, religions, and cultures.
But compassion can also be suppressed under the influence of "enemy"-
stereotypes.

In addition to the affectional and the rational-ethical aspects of compassion there is also a third dimension: the voluntative. As the parable of
the Good Samaritan shows, compassion as co-suffering or vicarious suffering does not lead to passive moaning, wailing and whining, but to a
spontaneous *activity* aiming to resolve the suffering and its causes. Compassion (German: "Mitleid") is more vigorous than sympathy and empathy
(German: "Mitgefühl"). It goes beyond understanding and literally moves
the person who is affected by it – moves that person both internally, as it
shapes his or her perception of the situation, and externally, as it impels
the person to take action. It impels the person thus affected to come to the
aid of the suffering Other so as to alleviate his or her distress. Thus compassion leads to the practice of neighbourly love: hospitality, social work,
engagement for the accused, the enslaved, the oppressed and the poor (cf.
Zechmeister 2007). These forms of active neighbourly love can be summed
up in the term "mercy", derived from the Latin *misericordia*. The feeling

---

[2] According to the Stoic understanding, the attitude of compassion ought not be
affected by emotional concernment. It is supposed to be a purely rational disposition.

of compassion – prompted by the misery (the suffering, the *passio*) of others – becomes the impulse for a saving, caring or helping activity. With a nearly irresistible power it pulls one towards an active engagement.[3]

The ethos of neighbourly love, as illustrated by the parable of the Good Samaritan, encompasses all three dimensions: the affection of compassion, its ethical attitude and its concrete practice. "Compassion" in the narrower sense refers only to the affectional dimension. In the broader and more important sense it extends throughout all three dimensions. It is that broader understanding of compassion as emotional concern, ethical attitude and practical engagement which makes it possible to avoid the problems which would arise if Christian ethics were grounded in compassion as a feeling – problems such as preferring to care for those who are close to me, since I *see* their suffering. Compassion as an attitude is not dependent on the "stirring of the bowels". That can of course serve as an important impulse for an act of neighbourly love but there can also be other, less stirring impulses. An openness for the needs of others refers not only to states of emergency or to violations of basic human rights, but concerns all needs, visible and invisible, of human beings – the needs of their bodies and souls, of their social relationships, of their communities.

The practice of neighbourly love must not be restricted to the treatment of the painful appearance of distress but has to be extended to the elimination of its causes. It is not only to be realized in the personal sphere as solidarity but also in the social arena as justice. From the perspective of Christian social ethics, the structures and functions of social institutions, political organizations and economical systems must be questioned as to whether or not they promote justice, fairness and a balance of interests. That is known as "structural agape".

In focussing on the relationship to the needy other we shouldn't forget to note that according to the Great Commandment of the Jewish and Christian tradition, which demands that we love God and the neighbour, "love" refers not only to the alleviation of distress and the compensation of deficiencies, but also to a fundamental acknowledgement of and a loving attention to that Other who is *not* in a miserable situation. There is then not only a 'negative' ("relieving from") but also a 'positive' ("doing good")

---

[3] For a more detailed elaboration of the notion of compassion: see Dalferth and Hunziker (2007), especially the introduction.

dimension. Especially the second of those dimensions is directed not only towards "Others" but also towards one's *own* person and community. That commandment calls upon me to love God and the neighbour "as thyself" (Lev 19:18; Deut 6:5; Mark 12:29–33; Matt 22:37–40; Luke 10:27; Gal 5:14; Jas 2:8). *Compassion as awareness* thus includes sensitivity to the needs of one's *own* self in all the various dimensions of his or her life. And both – the love of my neighbour and the love of myself – are rooted in God's love.

According to the first Epistle of John, God's very essence is love (4:8,16). The creature is called to respond to as well as to correspond to that love – in the relationship with God, with him- or herself, with other creatures and indeed with created reality as a whole. *Being-in-agape* is the utterly foundational characteristic of Christian existence, and as such it must then impact upon the Christian's most fundamental ways of seeing and find expression in his or her behaviour. The one side of agape is empathy and compassion, the other side practical caring. The mandate for self-giving service is set forth in Mark 10:42–45.

In the next part of my paper I would like to explore the importance of compassion as a core-element of Christian ethics in the encounter of people from different religious backgrounds.

II. Compassion as a motif for interreligious dialogue

Let me again return to the parable of the Good Samaritan. Although the Samaritans claimed descent from a group of the people of Israel at the time of the Babylonian Exile, their religious tradition differed from that of later mainline Judaism which looked upon them as ethnically, culturally and religiously inferior and impure. Pious Jews despised them and shunned all contact with them. For their part, the Samaritans accused the Jews of aberration from the Torah. Thus the parable of the Good Samaritan narrates the story of an encounter of persons belonging to different religious communities – both of which claimed superiority over the other. It is addressed to the Jews, represented by members of two distinguished groups – a priest and a Levite – whose members are expected to follow the commandment of neighbourly love in a particularly notable way. The parable tells them that it is precisely the heretic Samaritan who is moved by compassion and behaves in accordance with the will of God. Thus the message of the parable, as we have seen above, is that the adequate expression of being in communion with God is not constituted in belonging to a certain people, culture or religion, but in the practicing of solidarity with the needy Other. Compassion relativizes and overrides all boundaries of ethnic, cultural or religious identities. The decisive response to God's love and to the "new being" (expressed in the symbol of eternal life), evoked by the salvific will of God, is neighbourly love.

That makes compassion such an important issue for the encounter of adherents of different religious traditions. Understood in the narrower sense delineated above compassion plays a central role only in those encounters which refer in one way or another to a situation of distress. But understood in the broader sense, compassion becomes the attitude of acknowledgement which constitutes dialogical relationships.

I will try to systematize the instances of interreligious encounters in which compassion – in both the narrower and the wider sense – comes into play:

- when the encounter is driven by the *needs* of the adherents of other religions whom I meet, or on my needs, or on the needs of others, i.e. third parties;
- when the encounter takes up the question of how to *understand* those needs and how to *act* in order to alleviate the sufferings caused by them;
- when the encounter is rooted in the *ethics* of the respective religious traditions and in the *spiritual motivations* for following that ethical orientation.

Compassion can lead to interreligious encounter and can become a central issue for dialogue and conjoint action. It can create a tradition-transcending basis for interreligious understanding and can radiate from there, planting and developing the seeds of neighbourly love in the hearts of the participants of the encounter and of those who then come to be included in the resulting solidarity.

There are at least six different forms of encounter between the adherents of religions:

- the *intellectual* theological exchange at conferences, where experts seek to deepen their understanding of the various religious traditions;

- the interreligious encounter in *everyday life*, where people strive to live in a neighbourly spirit, sharing their problems and preoccupations;
- the *spiritual* communion, where people come together in prayer, contemplation, meditation and worship;
- the *ethical* dialogue of *action*, in which people collaborate for the improvement of living-conditions, for liberation and justice;
- the *interior* dialogue of a person with other religious traditions;
- the dialogue *about* dialogue, in which the possibilities, forms and difficulties of interreligious encounters are discussed.

The experience of compassion can and ought to become the emotional impetus for the dialogue of action (cf. Gilman 2003). In the case of the Good Samaritan the experience initiated a unilateral action, but it might also be a bi- or multilateral activity among members of different religious traditions working together to assist people in distress. In addition to single spontaneous interventions in acute states of emergency, continuous activity in fighting against poverty, illiteracy, and insufficient medical care is essential.

Hans Küng's Project World Ethos calls for an interreligious cooperation for the sake of humanity in the face of global challenges and responsibilities. This approach brackets off the different *theological* foundations upon which the basic ethical commandments of the world-religions are based. It restricts its focus to a common denominator in the moral instructions of the religious traditions. The project strives for a fourfold commitment capable of sustaining interreligious cooperation:

- the commitment to a culture of non-violence and respect for life;
- the commitment to a culture of solidarity and a just economic order;
- the commitment to a culture of tolerance and a life of truthfulness;
- and the commitment to a culture of equal rights and partnership between men and women.

These commitments follow from the ethos of neighbourly love. The question is: What might be the motivation for nurturing them and living out what they envision? The "Declaration Toward a Global Ethic" appeals to a "conversion of the heart"[4] in terms of a new consciousness created and

---

[4] www.weltethos.org/ Decl_english.pdf, page 14.

fostered by the religions. This is the consciousness of compassion – compassion in the broader understanding which goes beyond its emotional dimension. It encompasses perception and understanding of the Other, and it leads to action. The conversion of the heart reaches further than the conversion of the bowels.

But in all religious traditions there are counter-forces working against the power of compassion – forces which drive back the empathy with the needy ethnic or religious Other and which restrict it to the members of one's own clan or community or nation or religion; forces which demand a distinction between the neighbour and the stranger; forces which cause mischief, sowing the spirit of separation and hostility.

Within the religious traditions those forces opposed to an attitude of universal compassion are nurtured by and expressed in the claim of the superiority of one's own tradition over against the others. For example, this claim leads to distinctions between those who are saved and those who still have to be saved; and if they then refuse to become saved they are condemned by God. Even in the New Testament there are harsh verdicts against Gentiles and Jews. In his Epistle to the Romans Paul dooms those Gentiles who addict themselves to ungodliness and unrighteousness (1:29–32). And in his First Epistle to the Thessalonians he fulminates in a similar way against the Jews (2:15f).

On the other hand we ought not to forget that Paul himself was a Jew and his struggle to incorporate the Gentiles and the Jews into the body of Christ was a consequence of his attempt to save them. Perhaps he would have understood this attempt as a fruit of compassion. What Robert C. Roberts says of Christianity in general, may be said of Paul: "Christians regard sin and being out of fellowship with God as the primary harm to which human beings are subject" (Roberts 2003: 123; cf. Roberts 2007).

That conviction can however lead to forms of compassion which need critical scrutiny. If for instance a Christian feels compassion (or properly speaking: pity) with a Hindu because he/she is alienated from God, then one must indeed ask if this is an appropriate application of compassion. Such an example indicates the importance of ethical reflection on the *nature* of the distress which evokes compassion. And it shows that the sentiment of compassion can be linked with paternalistic attitudes, with attempts to convert people from other faith-traditions with claims for the superiority of one's own religious path or ethical preference. The ethical

mind-set of a person or community is closely associated with religious beliefs – in the case of my example: with the question as to how God's salvific
will and action is related to other religions. This issue is discussed in the
so-called "theology of religions".[5]

The ethical reflection on compassion must itself become an issue of
interreligious dialogue.[6] Dialogue rests upon the principle of mutuality. As
opposed to that, compassion is uni-directional; as an emotion, it is tied
to a subject-object relation: a person feels compassion for another sentient
being. The dialogical principle on the other hand calls for making the other
person a subject. It transfers the I-He/She-relation into an I-You-relation.

The implicit ethos of dialogue requires each participant to inquire into
the self-understanding of the other person, and gives this other person the
opportunity to articulate a personal view of his/her situation. It may be
the case that the other feels comfortable with what for me seems to be a
very uncomfortable, distressful situation which had evoked my compassion. Now it may be that this person is deluded about his or her real needs,
but it may also be that I have simply taken my own understanding of "well-
being" and absolutized it for all.

Only in a dialogical encounter can one find out how the other is experiencing a situation which to me appears distressing. Only in a dialogical encounter can one find out whether compassion is the appropriate response,
and if so, what practical activity should be undertaken to change the situation. Compassion is a strong motive for spontaneous charity but it needs
to be framed by ethical reflection and by dialogue, by the inner voice of
my ethical orientation and by the voice of the other. The normative orientation can not and ought not rely only on affections. It needs ethical
discourse and it needs to listen to the *self*-articulation of those for whose
sake I feel compassion. Each "other" bears his or her own normativity, and
a dialogue with him/her brings that into play. Compassion and dialogue
are two poles of an ellipse, and though tension may arise between them,
they actually belong together.

---

[5]   For further reading see: Bernhardt (1994) and Bernhardt (2006).

[6]   As it was undertaken by the conference "Care and Compassion. Methods for Sharing Values across Cultures and Religions", organized by globethics.net (Third International Conference, 24-29 January 2009, Nairobi, Kenya).

References

Bernhardt, R., 1994: *Christianity Without Absolutes*, London.

—, 2006: *Ende des Dialogs? Die Begegnung der Religionen und ihre theologische Reflexion* (Beiträge zu einer Theologie der Religionen 2), Zürich.

Blum, L., 1980: Compassion, in: A. O. Rorty (ed): *Explaining Emotions*, Berkeley.

Dalferth, I.U. and A. Hunziker (eds), 2007: *Mitleid. Konkretionen eines strittigen Konzepts*, Tübingen.

Evers, D., 2007: The Other as Neighbor. Theological Consideration, in: Dalferth and Hunziker (2007), 197–218.

Gilman, J.E., 2003: Whose God? Which Religion? Compassion as the Heart of Interreligious Cooperation, *Journal of Ecumenical Studies* 40 (2003), 267–295.

Roberts, R.C., 2003: *Emotions. An Essay in Aid of Moral Psychology*, Cambridge.

—, 2007: Compassion as an Emotion and Virtue, in: Dalferth and Hunziker (2007), 119–137.

Zechmeister, M. (ed), 2007: *Compassion: Außerhalb der Armen kein Heil. Theologische Korrektive im Globalisierungsprozess* (Religion – Geschichte – Gesellschaft, vol. 43), Münster.

8. Chapter

Compassion in Islam – Theology and History

Asghar Ali Engineer

ISLAM IS GENERALLY ASSOCIATED with Jihad. But it is more due to its history than its theology. It is interesting to note that while jihad in Islam is more historical than theological, compassion, on the other hand, is more theological than historical. The very opening of Qur'an, the holy book of Islam is with *Bism Allahir Rahmanir Rahim* i.e. I begin in the name of Allah who is Compassionate and Merciful.

Thus it will be seen that Compassion is one of the names of Allah and it is among the most popular names of Allah. Muslims always begin their name with this incantation i.e. 'I begin in the name of Allah who is Compassionate and Merciful'. A Muslim, who worships Allah has to be compassionate in his own behavior else his/her worship would not be complete. There are four key values in Qur'an which are repeatedly emphasized are: Justice ('adl), benevolence (ihsan), compassion (rahmah) and wisdom (hikmah) and compassion is one of them. Jihad, on the other hand, is not value but an instrument to realize certain objectives.

The Prophet of Islam too is described in Qur'an as *rahmat lil 'alamin* i.e. mercy of the worlds. Since Prophet is messenger of Allah he too has to represent His virtues on earth. Allah is perfect and so His Prophet has to be a perfect human being imbibing all the attributes of Allah. So other believers (*mu'minun*) also must, with all their limitations, imbibe these virtues.

A believer, who is not compassionate within possible human limits, is no believer at all. A true believer has to imbibe all those values represented by Allah and His Messenger. In other words Qur'an and sunnah (Prophet's sayings and doing) are binding on all Muslims and there is complete consensus on it among all Muslim theologians belonging to all sects of Islam.

Prophet lived in such historical situation and socio-political conjunction that occasionally he had to take to arms to defend himself and his community but this historical necessity cannot be counted as obligatory or value-oriented. At the most it can be called necessity-oriented. Al-Qaeda and some similar groups representing a miniscule minority among Muslims, are projecting jihad as if it is central value and obligatory. It is total falsification of teachings of Islam.

Let us remember necessity is situational and values are transcendent; necessity may compel human beings to do things which may not be strictly speaking desirable but values make society more *humane.* War, may become necessity at times but results in bloodshed and destruction and needs to be avoided as much as possible. Values, on the other hand, help purposefully construct society and are eternal.

It was due to historical necessity on one hand, and vested interests which used concept of jihad in a way that it appeared to be central to Islam where as values like compassion remained confined to one section of society represented by Sufis and weaker sections and hence never appeared on the pages of history which are reserved for the ruling classes. As we all know we read more about ruling classes in history than the ruled. And what rulers and ruling classes do is interest-oriented rather than value-oriented and it is for this reason that pages of history are red with blood.

Prophet's life history is full of value-oriented incidents but even biographers of the Prophet like Ibn-e-ishaq or Ibne Hisham have focused more on battles and wars than these events which would project the Prophet in true light. Prophet's name Muhammad (the praised one) was not because of his wars but because of his human qualities and the Prophet came to be known as Muhammad much before he became head of the community.

These virtues were his truthfulness, wisdom and compassion. He loved justice and hence formed an organization called *Hizb-al-fudul* to help the victims of injustices in his society. He himself was an orphan and had suffered many tribulations in life and had great sympathy for the weaker sections of society he lived in. All this became part of his divine message also.

Allah chooses His prophets from among the weaker sections of society as only such persons can be value-oriented as they know importance

of human values in life as against rulers and ruling classes who happen
to be interest-oriented. Thus one would see in Qur'an that all prophets
mentioned with the exception of David and Solomon (Daud and Suleman)
(who were rulers) happen to be from weaker sections of society.

It is prophets from this section of society who can communicate with
great conviction the divine message of truth, justice, benevolence, love,
compassion, human dignity and equality. All prophets of Allah brought
these values and exemplified them through their personal life. Prophet of
Islam too was embodiment of these values, particularly compassion. There
are numerous incidents from his life which show his compassionate approach towards fellow human beings irrespective of religion or station in
life.

Once a woman was bought to his presence and was told she is sinner
and must be punished. The Prophet, instead of asking her about her sins,
asked her what act of compassion she had done to any fellow being. She
said I cannot recall any act of good towards any other human being. She
reflected and said no I can't recall any such incident. The Prophet again
asked her whether you have helped any living being?

The woman thought for a while and said, yes, once a dog was thirsty
and there was some water in a pit he was unable to reach with his tongue.
I took pity on the dog, took off my sock and fetched some water from the
pit and gave it to the dog. The Prophet said go Allah will forgive all your
sin for his act of compassion towards an animal.

A frail and sick person came to the Prophet and said I have committed a grave sin, please punish me. Prophet asked him what sin have you
committed? Thereupon the person said I was sick and a woman came to
inquire of my health and I committed an act of sin with her. Please punish
me otherwise Allah will punish me eternally in the world hereafter. The
Prophet once again asked him if you really did this to the woman so as to
give him one more chance of denying. But the person persisted.

Since this person was too weak Prophet did not want to punish him
with hundred lashes which is the Qur'anic punishment for adultery. Prophet
thought for a while and asked hundred branches of palm date tree to be
brought, he tied them together and delivered one soft blow and told the
person go you have met with your punishment.

There is another often repeated story of a Jewish woman who sued
to throw garbage on the Prophet whenever he passed through that way.

When no garbage was thrown one day he inquired about the woman and was told she was sick. He went to her house to inquire about her health and prayed for her recovery. She of course was overwhelmed with this gesture of the Prophet and converted to Islam.

Needless to say it was not Prophet's intention to convert her but to show his deep personal concern for her illness. Had he not been compassionate he would not done that. These stories make it clear that the Prophet of Islam felt others sufferings as his own and would try to do whatever he could to lessen or remove these sufferings. It is strikingly like concept of *dukkha* in the Buddhist tradition and removal of *dukkha* is an act of religion.

Forgiveness is another quality essential for a compassionate behavior. Allah thus repeatedly described as *Ghafurur Rahim* (Forgiver and Merciful) in the Qur'an. He is not so much as Punisher but Forgiver. Sincere repentance (*taubah*) on the part of human beings leads to forgiveness of Allah.

The Prophet too was great forgiver. As far as possible he would forgive even worst of his enemies. When he conquered Mecca without shedding a drop of blood, he declared he would not punish anyone provided they did not fight and gave up arms. His enemies who had indulged in inhuman persecution of the Prophet and his companions, feared for the worst but were pleasantly surprised that Prophet pardoned all of them.

Abu Sufyan and his wife Hinda who were in the forefront of persecuting the Prophet and his companions and Hinda had chewed liver of his uncle Hamza who was most dear to him, were also pardoned. There can be hardly better example of forgiveness and compassion. And think of Arab society with all its tribal customs which considered *qisas* (retaliation in equal measure) a basic necessity. The whole society considered doctrine of *qisasi* central in the absence of any law enforcing agency.

Various Qur'an did sanction the doctrine of *qisas* (as there was no law enforcing machinery) but made it clear that forgiveness and compassion to the offender are superior values and who would practice these values if not the Prophet? He practiced them as the human exemplifier. Thus the Prophet did not teach anything but practiced it himself in most trying conditions. To forgive his worst enemies in Mecca was most challenging and no one would have complained if the Prophet had sought revenge. It was the norm of that society. But the Prophet wanted to establish superiority of higher values.

In Islamic world then there were two parallel streams and together they constituted Islamic mainstream. These two streams were socio-political stream and Sufi stream and both these stream had their own respective understanding of jihad. The socio-political stream which consisted of ruling and upper classes and on the other Sufis who got support mainly from weaker sections of society though part of the ruling class also had faith in Sufi saints due to their popularity among masses of people.

While the ruling classes understood by jihad defense of Islamic state and expansion of limits of Islamic state. A section of theologians depended for their sustenance on the ruling classes and hence their discourse on jihad was mainly to promote interests of ruling classes. Thus the large part of theological discourse on jihad supported the point of view of ruling classes and they defended jihad in the sense of military operations.

Jihad, on the other hand, meant inner struggle to suppress desires and cultivate virtues of patience (sabr) and reliance on Allah (tavakkul), for the sufi stream of Islam. There was'nt much support for war and political struggle among the sufi saints. The sufi saints tried to cultivate what Qur'an calls *nafs-e-mutmainna* (the contented soul) and not *nafs-e-ammarah* (desiring soul). Since it requires great deal of struggle to cultivate *nafs-e-mutmainnah* it was real jihad for sufi stream of Islam.

And let us remember it is *nafs-e-mutmainna* (contented soul) which also creates attitude of compassion. A grabbing and greedy soul which is *nafs-e-ammarah* can never show compassion towards the suffering of others and ruling classes and their supporters have this kind of soul as their greed can be fulfilled only by inflicting suffering on others. Thus it will be seen that jihad in the Qur'an is not in absolute sense of war or fighting against kafirs as usually understood.

Jihad is, on the other hand, layered concept and has been interpreted very differently by different classes of Muslims. Jihad is mainly spiritual and the Prophet of Islam had very complex kind of challenges both material and spiritual and hence he and his companions used jihad in both material and spiritual senses. However, its centrality lay in spiritual struggle and Sufis were basically enchanted by spiritual struggle of the Prophet and hence jihad for them was a supreme and most challenging struggle to suppress *nafs-e-ammarah (desiring* soul) and hence from them jihad had significance as a spiritual struggle.

Sufis had very caring and sharing attitude which is an important ingredient of compassion. They expressed their solidarity with suffering people and weaker sections of society and that is why thousands of people had great reverence for them. Though they received lot of money from their devotees including members of ruling classes, they never spent it on their self.

They used to open what is called *langar* i.e. a common kitchen where anyone irrespective of caste and creed could eat any time of the day. Thus they had very compassionate attitude towards suffering people. They derived their inspiration from a *hadis-e-qudsi* (a divine hadis) which is as follows: Allah would ask on the Day of Judgment "I was hungry and you did not feed me, I was thirsty and you did not quench my thirst and I was naked and you did not clothe me. The person being held to account would say O! Allah you are the Provider of food how could I feed you? Allah would say my servant (abd) was hungry and you did not feed him. If a human person is hungry as if I am hungry and if a human person is thirsty as if I am thirsty, and if a human person is naked as if I am naked." Thus the Sufis always saw to it that any human being who came to them should not go back hungry. They would do everything possible to feed him/her.

They would even go hungry and feed the person who happened to be hungry. And this compassion extended to even animals and plants. The Prophet once saw a donkey who was indentured on its face. He berated its owner that you have no compassion for this poor animal. You have disfigured its face. The owner said it is required for identifying the animal. Prophet told him at least do not disfigured its face and do it on some other part of the animal.

Sufi Junaid once say an ant crawling in his room. He got worried that someone would trample it underfoot and ant will be killed. He thought for a moment how to save its life. He saw a container containing wheat flour lying in the room. He gently lifted ant and put it in the container. Such was the compassion of Sufis towards human beings, animals and even an ant.

Compassion is highly necessary for sustenance of life on this earth. A compassionate approach only can make our life rich. It is greed which makes human beings ruthless towards others as one can fulfill once greed only by inflicting suffering on others. For a compassionate person thus it is necessary to lead need-based life, not greed-based life. The Qur'an exhorts believers to give away their surplus to the needy people (2:219).

Qur'an also levies a tithe on Muslims called zakat which has to be spent on orphans, widows, poor, needy, wayfarers and for releasing of prisoners. All these are helpless sections of society and hence need our compassion. It is obligatory for all Muslims to spend of their wealth on these helpless sections of society. It is not possible without having compassion towards them.

Thus it is compassion which makes us real human being. A human being who is not sensitive towards suffering of fellow human beings or animals and plants cannot be human being indeed. Thus there is constant struggle between greed and need and generally it is greed which triumphs and result is lot of suffering of large number of human beings on earth.

We can triumph over greed only through compassion. In fact all religions want to enrich our spiritual life and thus teach compassion. It is no religion which does not teach compassion. No religion promotes greed. But history of that religion is often history of its ruling classes and ruling classes are overpowered by greed for power and self and thus often we find lot of bloodshed and wars in history of these religions including that of Islam.

However there is always a parallel stream which is never highlighted in history which is that of Sufis and saints engaged not in struggle for power but struggle to overpower, over power their desire and greed and cultivate compassionate attitude towards others. It is this section of people who are salt of life and who find eternal reverence in the hearts people, though not in their history.

We are also increasingly becoming insensitive to suffering of our own climate. We want to live greedy life and do not mind even destroying our climate. It is our over consumption which is leading to destruction of our climate and our sensitivity towards it. Thus we have to cultivate an attitude of compassion towards our climate also. Reducing our consumption would achieve two purposes: one, helping needy people on earth who are deprived of their just right to exist and secondly, would help normalize our climate.

Thus compassion towards others suffering can result in enriching our life both materially and spiritually. Today ours is consumer society and whole emphasis is on consumption and the capitalist system draws its dynamism from ever increasing consumption and it is sought to be boosted through high-powered advertisement. This race forever increasing consumption has made us, increasingly insensitive, towards other's suffering.

It is not easy to reduce our consumption as a whole though some individual may succeed in doing that. We have to carefully cultivate the attitude of compassion towards suffering of others to achieve this objective. According to me religion can become a rich resource for cultivating compassion in human beings. This can happen only when our understanding of religion is transformed by religious leaders.

Our understanding of religion is entirely ritual centered today. We have to go beyond rituals and religion should be our active guide for transforming our inner self, a contented inner being wholly occupied with values like love, selflessness, compassion and truthfulness. This in fact is real religiosity, not merely performing certain rituals. This also often leads to competitive religiosity and tension between communities.

Qur'an repeatedly talks of *istibaq al-khayrat* i.e. excelling each other in good deeds and what are good deeds, if not deeds based on these values of love, compassion and truthfulness. The Prophet is reported to have said that it is more meritorious to feed a hungry widow than pray whole night. Thus compassion towards a hungry soul is more important than prayer. Allah hardly needs our prayer.

And actually prayer and fasting has also been prescribed to cultivate with these values, not because Allah needs them. Rituals are a means to an end, not an end in themselves but we have reduced them to an end itself. We must urgently revise our attitude towards ritual-oriented religion and replace it with value-oriented one, if we have to reduce suffering of humanity. Buddhism and Islam both greatly compliment each other in cultivating compassion among their followers. Christianity and Hinduism too with their emphasis on love and non-violence can be valued associates and we can transform our world. Will these religions join hands to reduce suffering of our earth?

9. Chapter

Compassion As A Shared Value: Indic Perspectives

Anindita N. Balslev

A SEARCH FOR SHARED VALUES in a global context certainly deserves priority in a collective agenda of projects that are to be deemed as critically important in our time. To discern common values, just as to construe common norms for collective behaviour, is an urgent venture today since all nations seem to be increasingly striving to share a common scientific technology irrespective of their specific cultural traditions.

At present, it is palpable that a common adoption of advanced technology has reduced the barriers of geographical distances enabling us to travel and communicate across the globe at a speed that is unprecedented, but this has at the same time also made it glaringly visible that we have not succeeded in bridging various forms of cultural distances in an adequate, let alone in a satisfactory manner. Under such precarious circumstances, we can hardly ignore the need to put some effort into crafting and nurturing a program with the view of identifying common values across cultures and arriving at a consensus with regard to norms of human transactions at various level. These indeed could be tremendously supportive for fostering a greater sense of human solidarity than what is there at present. If we succeed in detecting the overlaps that is already at hand in our sense of values while enjoying the enriching influence of cultural diversity, we can surely hope to agree with more ease about some of the regulative principles that are now missing in the practical sphere of action in the public space.

Looking at various socio-ethical norms in varied cultural soils, it is indeed noticeable that these are very largely derived from the conceptual resources that stem from the prevailing religious traditions. This seems to be so even when the present population residing in such cultures seek to distance itself from the 'religious' and claim to be be 'secular' in making various sorts of public commitments with regard to all current affairs. However, no matter how astonishing that may sound to the skeptical ears, the world-religions remain to this day the principal and primary sources from which the largest aggregates of humanity receive guidance and draw a sense of collective identity. This is why the question of values associated with world-religions is a matter that can be side-tracked in the public space only to our peril. A true appreciation of common values and norms – be these something to be 'found' or 'made' - is to be considered as vital at various levels of social interactions. A public recognition of these values, it may be expected, would not only have great impact on social psychology in multi-ethnic milieus that are preponderant today but would also have the potentials of influencing various socio-political agendas in global context paving the way for peace and harmony.

Unfortunately, despite our keen awareness of the multi-religious dimension of the contemporary global scenario, we do not seem to fully acknowledge the importance of public participation in an endeavor that could bridge the gap of knowledge that is there in the public space with regard to the 'other' religious traditions than our own. If we could convince ourselves, as a few have tried to do without success, that we are actually living in a post-religious era, the effort to bring about an authentic encounter of world-religions could be said to be of lesser significance. It is, however evident that this is not the case. On the contrary, it is quite obvious that the current scenario is one in which despite all the ongoing deliberations on the topics of modernity and secularism, the presence of the plurality of world-religions is vibrant, perhaps more so in places where the traditions are fully alive than in others, but nowhere it seems to be absent. This seems to be the case even where conscious effort was made in the past to oust a religion, since its resurgence has shown that it has been hardly treated with indifference by the participants of the said tradition.

Regrettably, however, we find that the presence of plurality of world-religions is treated even today - unquestionably no less than before - more as a divisive force than as a collective resource. This state of affairs right away calls for correction or else we are to continue to inflict pain and suffering on each other in the name of the 'otherness' of the other religious traditions, perhaps by making use of the present-day advanced technology for further feeding the system of violence. It is time to realize that when we pay lip service to the cause of secularism, while often confusing religious affiliations to distinct communities as various forms of communalism, we tend to overlook the fact that the world-religions do unanimously recommend such common values as practice of compassion, while largely condemning and renouncing violence. If more discussion is called for on these issues, it shows that what we need is a bona fide meeting of world-religions where the participants of these traditions have the possibility of engaging in open conversation on themes of common concern. It has to be acknowledged that such an endeavor is no less significant than any other measures earnestly conceived for the purpose of reducing and eliminating large scale conflict. At a time when physical distances between 'we' and 'they' diminish day by day, it is crucially imperative that some effective tools are conceived where modern technology can play a role to better inform members of any one of the given traditions about the traditions of 'others' than it has been the case so far. Recall the pertinent statement made by Sarvepalli Radhakrishnan (a well-known philosopher, a politician, served as the second President of India) who fittingly remarked that 'no one is so vain about his own religion as the one who knows of no other'.

Let us keep in mind that if the twentieth century has said to be the bloodiest in the recorded history of humankind, there are ominous signs that the twenty-first century may turn out to be much worse in which the question of religion may well be further abused. Sometimes it seems that precisely due to the lack of a clear perception of common values that are cherished across cultural traditions that our present-day multi-religious situation is seen more as a cause for strife than as a vibrant starting place that could be explored with the hope of creating better understanding among diverse groups. Surely, skeptics may still ask: Are there really common values? Is compassion, for example, truly a value that all traditions share? The answer to such a question – note - requires not any imagination but knowledge of other traditions. In other words, this search for common values not only demands greater participation in each other's tradition but also a preparedness to unlearn some of our pre-conceived, ill-informed prejudices.

No doubt a range of questions appear before us. We are tempted to ask what this idea of compassion is all about, how has it been analyzed and interpreted in the cognitive discourses that are associated especially with different world-religions? Even, one can be more philosophical and wonder what underlies the fabric of the human situation that 'compassion' as a value is generally recommended across the board? Moreover, from the angle of the actual teachings documented in various religious discourses, the insistence 'seems to be' not only simply on cultivating a compassionate attitude but on boldly putting the idea into action, implementing it in all arenas of life, in all forms of human relationships. The world-religions seem to regard the practice of compassion NOT as an option but as an obligation. I keep on using the phrase 'seem to be' since usually our knowledge is limited to one or two world-religions, while regarding the rest it is mostly drawn from scanty information, imagination and heresy.

As it stands, it is possible that some of us tend to think of compassion as a common value, perhaps because we frequently come across in various religious narratives depictions of exalted personalities who are regarded as the actual parishioners of compassion. Moreover, we find that these traditions universally acclaim that such rare individuals have thereby not only transformed their own lives but also those of people around them. Be these actual historical retellings, anecdotes or legends, the fact is that we recognize in these accounts something elevating and compelling, since the lives and conduct of such compassionate individuals remind us about the inescapable normative dimension of human existence. These stories have not only enriched the specific traditions where these have stemmed from but these certainly have a universal appeal. We begin to sense that there are common values. Most importantly, these narratives have the power to make us keenly aware of the fact that it is precisely *due to the lack of compassionate behaviour on our part that human-suffering has turned out to be largely man-made.*

Indeed, the varied and the rich conceptual contents entailed in the notion of compassion – irrespective of whether these are present in the discourses of various philosophico-religious or in secular moral traditions - are of great interest not only in the theory-making front in the domain of ethics, but are also of profound significance in the practical sphere of human exchanges, both on individual and collective plane. Undeniably, familiarity with various cross-cultural interpretations of these ideas are informative and inspiring in countless ways, just as these are helpful for disclosing the shared values of all humanity.

It is tempting to hope that as we gradually construe a common frame of enquiry with the specific intention of noting the overlaps, notwithstanding the differences in the treatment of the normative principles, we will be better prepared to ascertain with heightened conviction whether or not there are common values. We will also – instead of making any assumption - learn to appreciate the diverse and variegated ways in which values in general are conceptually construed in the literature of the major traditions, such as the Indic and the Abrahamic. To be able to do away with stereotypical demarcations between 'we' and 'they', as mentioned before, is very likely to bestow benevolent influence on designing future course of public policy-making in more ways than can even be envisioned today.

As it stands now, we all know that distortions of religious ideas are not difficult to come across. This may well be - more often than not – due to a general deficiency of knowledge about each other's traditions. The dangerous consequence of this state of affairs has been that 'imaginary differences' have helped, as it were, to legitimize the great divide between 'we' and 'they'. A collective will is necessary to change that climate which has proved both socially and politically harmful. As I have said elsewhere, knowledge of real differences do not provoke us to demonize the 'otherness' of the other. On the contrary, it makes it possible for us to obtain a more balanced view of things, enabling us to identify what we still hold in common despite these differences. An authentic search for common values precisely entails such a process.

There is little doubt in my mind that an effective way to play down the abuse of religious differences which have cruel consequences in the hands of imaginative and malevolent politicians and even preachers, is to provide the adherents of various world-religions opportunities to learn about each others' tradition. Let us face the question squarely: Has sufficient effort been made so far via educational institutions and media for discerning and propagating what is 'shared' in the teachings and preachings of Hinduism, Buddhism, Jainism, Christianity, Judaism and Islam as well as in other faiths and traditions besides these? Will it make any difference if we learn to look at the diverse world-religions as an untapped resource yet to be explored for our common good or if we could figure out in collaboration how our shared values could be implemented in this conflict-ridden planet for the sake of achieving greater social harmony?

Now let me turn to the Upanisadic and the Buddhist traditions and seek to comprehend how the idea of compassion has been played out in the philosophical literature and note its continued relevance in contemporary context. Existing documents show that the question of values in general, including the idea of compassion/ Karuna, plays a vital role in the Indic thought traditions – theistic and non-theistic – inducing deep philosophical reflections for centuries. Both the Hindu and the Buddhist thinkers have dealt with the many facets of the notion of compassion with considerable philosophical dexterity. Although it will not be possible to go into detail, mention must be made of the Jaina thinkers as well for their profound exploration of the notion of Ahimsa or non-violence that has, like the idea of Daya or kindness/mercy, overlapping contents with the idea of Karuna or compassion. It is interesting to mention here that it has been re-peatedly urged by the thinkers of these traditions that all these great vows and values like compassion (Karuna), non-violence (Ahimsa) and kindness (Daya), need to be practiced in speech, thought and action (Kaya-mana-vakya). In the Indic traditions, attempts have been made to comprehend these ideas in cognitive, emotive and volitional terms. These elaborations are significant in social as well as in stereological contexts.

Although in common parlance, there are clearly overlaps in the way the words 'Daya' (mercy), Ahimsa (non-violence) and Karuna (compas-sion) are employed, in various literature these are sometimes used even interchangeably. However, some of the philosophical texts demonstrate a keener sense of sophistications and construe the meanings of these words, by making more sharp formulations of each of these concepts. Thus, it is fascinating to read the discussions in the commentaries, sub-commentaries of the Yoga-Sutra on why compassion or Karuna is highlighted as the high-est in the scale of virtues and vows that are recommended. The thinkers who hold Karuna to be the highest value point out that great as the value of 'Ahimsa' may be, it has nevertheless a negative tinge, as the very construal of the word A-himsa/non-violence literally suggests. The literal meaning, they say, primarily hinges upon prohibiting to do violence (A-himsa). On the other hand, 'Daya' i.e.mercy or kindness, is defined as the volition to remove the suffering of others (Paraduhkhamocana-.iccha). Again, it has been commented that although 'Daya' undoubtedly entails a benevolent and deep feeling, it still entails an attitude where, as it were, the recipients of mercy are perceived as being in an inferior situation. In other words, the recipients are seen as being in a state of deprivation compared to the agents upon whom it is incumbent to practice Daya. In contrast to these, it has been claimed that 'Karuna' is a positive value. Unlike Ahimsa, it is not just refraining from a certain undesirable practice; unlike Daya, it does not bear any suggestion to perceive its objects as in any sense less than oneself.

It is especially noteworthy that in the Yoga tradition, for example, it has been repeatedly said that without the attainment of serenity and one-pointedness (ekagrata), the pursuit of Yoga is not possible. Moreover, it is also clearly mentioned that purification of the mind (Citta-parikarma) is necessary for getting rid of a disturbed state of mind since this hinders concentration. Now the question that arises here is how exactly does one attain that purification? The text itself provides the answer to that question. It is said that apart from meditation on God (Isvara.pranidhana), 'the mind becomes tranquil by the cultivation of amity, compassion, goodwill and indifference towards those who are happy, miserable, virtuous and vicious respectively'. (cf. Maitri-karuna-muditopeksanam sukhaduhkhapunyapunyavisayanam bhavanatascittaprasadanam)

Let us specifically focus on what actually has been said with regard to the idea of compassion as this is most relevant for the sake of our present enquiry. One significant question that arises is 'on whom should compassion be bestowed?' The answer that is offered in the well-known commentary byVyasa is that an aspirant of Yoga needs to practice compassion toward all those who are suffering (cf. 'Duhkhitesu Karunam').

Interestingly, more clarity is demanded by the interlocutors about not only what the notion of Karuna really entails but also with regard to the referent of the word 'duhkhi' or sufferer. In other words, since it is recommended that compassion must be shown toward the duhkhis or the persons who are undergoing suffering, it is asked, precisely who are these sufferers ('duhkhis') that the text is referring to? Does this mean that compassion is to be practiced only when we find that our friends and relatives are undergoing suffering? Collectively speaking, the question can be posed as to whether this recommendation is designed exclusively for our allies, with whom we have clearly drawn out pacts for guarding our common interests, so that we think it to be worthwhile to bring help when they and only they seem to suffer – say from flood or famine, or from civil war or when being attacked from outside, whereas we can simply remain indifferent if these happen to 'others' – no matter how this 'otherness' is construed?

Texts belonging to the tradition amplify the enquiry by documenting the conversation. One commentator answers that question by emphasizing that the word 'Duhkhi' (sufferer) does not imply only those who are considered to be friends; what is meant here by that word includes both friends and not-friends ('mitra' and 'amitra'). The word 'not-friends' (a-mitra) refers not only to those who are indifferent to us but also our opponents and enemies.

Let me summarise the major purpose of this discussion as there are several important points to appreciate. Firstly, emphasis is laid on the fact that it is through practice of compassion, one gradually transcends the barrier between the self and the other, between we and they. Secondly, this practice also needs to be seen as one of the primary means for overcoming all tendencies to vile others (para-apakara). Finally, a sincere cultivation of Karuna in speech, thought and action, is not only to be seen as having an exclusively socio-ethical goal. It is indeed an integral and indispensable part of the process that leads to a state of one-pointedness (ekagrata). Unless and until one achieves this one-pointed concentration, it is insisted, discriminatory knowledge (viveka-jnana) that alone finally leads to Freedom(Kaivalya/Mukti) cannot arise. In this way, the practice of compassion also serves the stereological goal.

In the Hindu conceptual world, the theistic schools within the Vedic tradition have explored the notions of compassion and grace with great acumen and sensitivity. The literature of the Bhakti-tradition has plenty of narrations with lofty ideals while referring to personal God, avatars (incarnations) and elevated humans who personify compassion. These demonstrate the importance attributed to those who are compassionate and tell about their far-reaching concerns for all those who are suffering. These relate about their strong resolve and willingness to help all without discrimination. Indeed, theses narratives are vehicles through which traditions speak to us and we need to share these narratives. Enormous research material is available on this profound topic for anyone who wishes to undertake to do a comprehensive work.

In brief, we find that these thinkers have not only wrestled with abstract questions, such as how the attainment of knowledge and practice of compassion are closely linked together on a conceptual level but have also engaged themselves in the task of how to translate these lofty ideas into agendas for action, indicating the ways it needs to be played out in diverse contexts in the world at large. It is worth recalling here the conversation that is recorded in the Bhagavad Gita(32/6). When Arjuna asks the question: 'Who is the greatest yogi?' The reply given to him by Sri Krishna is that 'one who perceives others to be the same as the self, who makes the happiness and suffering of others his own is the greatest yogi'. This response hardly needs any further elaboration to be appreciated.

Note that it is not only the advocates of various theistic schools but also the Advaitins, who propounded the idea of the ontological non-duality of consciousness, have dealt with the idea from their respective perspectives. In various historical narratives, one encounters varied examples of what compassion really entails in day-to-day life in the context of the philosophy of Advaita Vedanta. However, mention must be made of a superb example of a massive agenda that was launched using the profound idea of non-duality along with its practical implications. This can be seen in the life and work of Swami Vivekananda – a name that easily comes to mind as one approaches the event of the Parliament of World Religions.

Swami Vivekananda, an enthusiastic interpreter of the Vedantic tradition in late 19th century strongly advocated that the aim of the Vedantic teaching was not only to go ahead and vigorously propagate the metaphysical message of non-duality or simply think that Vedanta is exclusively for other-worldly purposes. Inspired by Vedanta, he was prompted to work tirelessly for an implementation of what he describes as 'Practical Vedanta'. 'To see the self in all' is to practice compassion. This has led to a movement that seeks to foster a program for social upliftment, which, he insisted, needs to be seen as an integral part of the teaching of Vedanta. This deserves special mention as it is one of the finest examples that demonstrate how to employ a value-oriented religious concept into the sphere of daily practical life for the benefit of all, but especially for those who are oppressed and marginalized.

Swami Vivekananda was deeply inspired by his Guru Shri Ramakrishna's teaching that 'a man whose 'stomach is empty', who is hungry cannot be expected to be righteous'. He appreciated the absurdity of preaching Vedantic thought in purely metaphysical terms to those who suffer from hunger and poverty. He taught that the Vedantic ideas are to be translated into projects for the betterment of collective life, especially for upliftment of those who are in distress. Advaita or non-dualism in thought must inspire compassion in practice. Those who are privileged to have the knowledge of the philosophy of Advaita Vedanta must not only share it with others but must translate it into action in this world itself.

Let us note carefully - the view that knowledge that is beneficial for all must be shared and applied - is a theme that appears in the Indic traditions over and over again in a variety of ways. Many of us are familiar with the way the Buddhist tradition recounts how prince Siddhartha attains enlightenment or bodhi. A number of texts describe - in slightly different versions - how immediately upon the dawning of his enlightenment, the Buddha pondered over the question whether to pass into Nirvana to which he was fully entitled or to still remain among those who are immersed in suffering and ignorance in order to preach. It is said that the Buddha could win over his initial hesitations and opted for the second of the two alternatives, indeed out of 'Karuna' or compassion for all living beings. By doing so, he emerges before us as an outstanding world-teacher. One comes across repeatedly in the literature the description that he was no 'tight-fisted' teacher. In other words, he shared his knowledge in an unreserving manner and did not hold back anything whatsoever that could be significant for the striving for Buddhahood. The texts refer to him with reverence as the 'compassionate one' who fully disclosed the path by following which it is possible for an aspirant to attain enlightenment. Conceptually, this compassionate attitude is better understood when one becomes familiar with the amazing idea of the 'unity of all beings' – a piece of wisdom which is worked out in great detail in the texts. This also lays bare at the same time why the sacred function of the Buddhas, the possessors of 'knowledge of equality' (Samatajnana) is to unceasingly, untiringly pursue to help free all creatures in bondage. This is a superb analysis that touches upon the crucial question regarding how exactly wisdom and compassion go hand in hand. Indeed, as one dwells on these reflections, one comes to perceive that these are two sides of the same coin. Recall that the Buddhist tradition has highlighted the notion of Tathagata -Garbha, that conveys the idea that the germ of Buddhahood is present everywhere. Moreover, it has been insisted upon that the striving for Buddhahood is entirely for manifesting that which is present in the seed-form.

These sort of textual narrations – be these historical or anecdotal – show that the idea and practice of compassion can be seen not only as having a clear stereological dimension to it but also as suggestive of the fact that unwillingness to share knowledge that can be beneficial for the other is a clear mark of lack of compassion. The contemporary relevance of holding such attitudes can be seen even in such cases where technological know-hows are withheld from those who could benefit from such knowledge. This is also to be taken as an example of lack of compassion.

Advocacy and practice of such compassionate approach in many practical matters are also exemplified in the case of some of the exceptional persons of our time as well. Recall, for example, the case of Norman Borlaug, the agricultural scientist, whose recent demise is a loss for all of us. His life's work provides us with an excellent illustration for demonstrating how scientific technology needs to be combined with a compassionate attitude in order to strive for peace in a profound and effective way. This is a mind-set which is worth emulating. When he received the Nobel peace prize, this great fighter against hunger did not forget to remind the world of the gruesome fact that for millions of people 'hunger has been a constant companion and starvation has all too often lurked in the nearby shadows'. Norman Borlaug observed boldly that 'The destiny of world civilization depended upon providing a decent standard of living for all'. It has been said that whenever any new invention was made in the field of agricultural science, he exclaimed 'take it to the farmer', intending that such a useful piece of knowledge must be shared with those who actually till the land.

Indeed, the absence of will in assisting a given specific group of populations where distress and disease dominate, the large-scale lethargy that allows grave situations to prevail longer than need be – as in the case of extreme poverty, of food- and water -crisis, victimizations of cruel customs and of the institution of war as well as by other oppressive social forces disclose far too often a tremendous lack of compassion on the part of those who could respond positively in such situations. These can sometimes be motivated by self-interest of a given community, in some other cases it might well be because our sense of community comes to get defined very narrowly, often due to the way artificial boundaries are drawn in the name of the 'otherness' of the other. Sometimes this lack of compassion towards others on our part is even sought to be justified by projecting the 'others' as being undeserving of compassion. Indeed, there is no dearth of examples when suffering is inflicted by exaggerating a sense of otherness along the lines of race, nationality, ethnicity, gender and religious group-identities. All these seem to play a considerable role in the game of dividing humanity into dominant and marginalized groups in diverse settings. Such scenarios are visible today within specific national as well as international contexts. Daily reports are available showing that the victims are often those who are on the other side of where political, economic and military power rests, so even when means for eradication of suffering are available, these are not employed in specific cases. In other words, to whom compassion should be extended for the amelioration of a given situation becomes purely a matter of decision for the mighty and not an ethical demand where a sense of human solidarity calls for a joint-action.

We need to ask ourselves whether it is conceivable that if world-religions were standing together today that this could be a major force in deterring us from such practices as selectively employing scientific technology for eradicating extreme poverty or eliminating certain diseases, or while dealing with issues of food and water crisis more effectively in certain regions than in other? We can further ask whether a properly informed compassionate science-religion program be of assistance to de-legitimize the institution of war that entails colossal wastage of intellectual and economic resources? Could that be helpful for seeking other alternatives for conflict-resolutions? After all, can a value-oriented scientific technology legitimize itself while serving the cause of violence?

It is likely that an authentic encounter of traditions will enable us to face together the challenge of uncovering what the world-religions are really calling upon us to do. As we become better informed, we will be more capable of grasping the shared messages that would en able us to detect distortions that are done in the name of any of the world-religions. It will be philosophically intriguing, for example, to know the answers from various traditions to such questions as asked earlier: 'Who do or do not deserve compassion'?

Answers from the Indic traditions are quite clear. One of the Buddhist texts, for example, clearly says that this great compassion of the Buddhas is so profound that it does not even brook with any such distinction as that between those who are said to be deserving compassion and those who are not. Moreover, it has been emphasized that this great compassion is not limited only to a specific period of time or by a bounded space. In other words, it is directed to all (not only to a chosen few) and it is a bestowal on humanity that continues for ages and ages. Indeed, the compassion of the Buddhas is not only for their contemporaries or only for their own kinsmen nor is it only for those few who alone can be said to deserve it. The 'great compassion' knows of no boundary of space and time, no gulf is acknowledged between the self and the other.

There are many such readings which bring out clearly the overlapping contents in the theoretical analysis of the notion and practice of Karuna that prevail within the Upanisadic and Buddhist traditions. Striking indeed is the fact that not only these traditions are unanimous in recognizing that this great value of Karuna is not just a fleeting sentiment but also in emphasizing that it is firmly based on knowledge. In the case of Advaita Vedanta, this is expressed as the knowledge of the non-dual self whereas in the case of Buddhism, it is entailed in the idea of unity of all beings. Both traditions agree that the exalted beings who truly practice compassion do it for the sake of all living beings without any discrimination and that there is no question of any self-seeking or egoistic goal that motivate or persuade them in this matter. When we read the relevant literature, it is hardly possible to overlook the overlaps in these traditions with regard to values despite that one is standing for Amerada (Upanisadic tradition) and the other, Anatmavada (Buddhist tradition).

In this connection, it is also significant to perceive that both the Tathagata in Buddhism as well as the Personal God/Isvara of Yoga are worshipped as Compassionate Teachers who show the path by following which ultimate freedom becomes possible for others. This is also why Isvara in Yoga literature is venerated as the ultimate teacher i.e. the Teacher of all teachers (Parama-Guru). Again, the idea of benign intention which is entailed in the practice of Karuna by the enlightened ones is particularly emphasized in these traditions. The well-known Buddhist philosopher Aryadeva writes: "No exertion or activity of the Buddhas is without meaning or purpose, their very breath is for the good and welfare of all beings".

Similarly, one comes across the idea of work born of unmotivated compassion in the Bhagavad Gita, where Sri Krishna says: 'There is nothing in all the three worlds which I do not already possess; nothing I have yet to acquire'.(22/3 - 25/3), implying that all His work is for the sake of benefit of humankind (loka-samgraha).

While winding up the discussion, it certainly seems to me that the extent to which it will be possible for us to detect the overlaps in the conceptual contents and to appreciate the thrust of such values as compassion in various traditions, it will become that much easier to grasp the practical import of the idea regardless of what other differences may distinguish these traditions. We will be inspired to mobilize our resources, our energy that befits a compassionate program based on scientific technology and inspired by religious achievements of the human race. In other words, this will enhance our capability to work out ways and means for removing a large part of human suffering that is essentially man-made.

At the end, let me observe once again that the opportunity that living in a technological civilization has opened up for all of us cannot be said to have been properly utilized until we will find out how to explore one of our greatest resource – the world-religions – for the good of all. It is high time to openly recognize that really not much progress has been made with regard to bridging cultural distances that thwart a mutual understanding among the adherents of diverse world-religions. Most tragic is that provocations to adopt violent attitudes toward adherents of different communities in the socio-political arena of collective life are even sought to be defended, overtly or covertly, in the name of world religions. Instead of falling prey to the provocation to continue to play these traditions against each other, let there be some collective will to engage in the positive task of promoting a sense for human solidarity in a global context in which the religions of the world can make significant contributions. It is by now quite evident that if we seek to take upon ourselves a sense of social responsibility and shared accountability for human suffering, the knowledge of the overlaps in the value-orientations among the teachings of the great world-religions will be helpful. The recommendation of a common value like compassion is suggestive of a path toward transcending the perpetual conflict between the good of one, good of some and the good of all.

Finally, it is time to acknowledge that our blindness to perceive the overlapping contents in value-orientations has to a large degree inhibited our capacity to create a harmonious world-community. To put it in a nutshell, to search for common values is to dare to go deeper into these traditions and grasp where lies the transformative power in each of these. Once compassion is recognized to be a shared value and we earnestly engage ourselves to translate it as a common project, it is likely to unleash a play of subtle forces and energies that will gradually influence the cognitive, the volitional as well as the emotional dimensions of our existence. We are then likely to create a new compassionate climate where human suffering will no longer be seen as man-made.

It is tempting to hope that those of us who have made the effort to be present at the Parliament of the World's Religions would constantly remain vigilant and remind all concerned that no matter whether we are dealing with the intricate scenarios of political conflicts or various forms of social injustice, or addressing issues of hunger and thirst, of energy and environment that all agenda of actions must proceed with respect for this shared value.

10. Chapter

Human Solidarity

LOKESH CHANDRA

THE MOST BEAUTIFUL PARADIGM OF LIFE is our loyalty to Humankind away from the yawning gap between God and the 'first man'. History counts victims of the buzz of God, the desolation of humane ideals because of theistic violence as a prime requisite, as theism bypasses Life in the dreams of an unknown and unseen Absolute.

Prof. Anindita Balslev has chosen a timely topic for our discussions: human solidarity. Humanism puts man in the centre of the intellectual and spiritual universe, wherein "human life" is the reference point of all thought, away from the civilising mission of various theologies. It is a revolt against the domination of the unseen abstruse. It is relativism, the opposite of every form of absolutism, that destroys the reality and truth of Life. In the maxim of Protagoras "man is the measure of all things". Genuine human needs are the seeking. Open-mindedness about a continuing human evolution ensures that Life is the Meaning of our existence. Humanism is against dehumanisation under the Absolutism of a God-based world-view where human life itself is "original sin". The claims of exclusive possession of a divine mandate to abolish existing freedoms of multiplicity of religious Systems and liberal cultures that are integral to local conditions, is fast becoming violence an a global scale and is destabilising societies.

I. Human Solidarity needs Homocentrism

The word 'human' is from *homo* 'man', it is based on *humus* 'earth', and it means an 'earthly being'. Even the Hebrew word *ādam* 'man' derives from *ādāmāh* 'ground'. It is in contrast to '*divine*' which is derived from Old Latin *deivos* 'god'. Man was conceived of as an emanation of the earth, that is, of terrestrial existence, of Life. Heaven was not his progenitor. Thus language assures the biocentric character of man, as contradistinguished from a heavenly father. A homocentric view guarantees the negation of fundamentalism and of absolutism. It is liberal, humanitarian, and prompts a practical approach to social, political and intellectual issues. It gives rise to a belief in human progress and a rejection of dogmatic authority. It is an emphasis on lasting human values. Humans can come together only in a pluralism where diversity and change are owned and respected.

Solid is one of the three common states of matter in physics (solid, liquid, gas). Its molecules are limited to vibrations about a fixed position. Solid has a definite shape but has vibrations that can begin to move rapidly until they break out of their fixed positions und the solid becomes a liquid. Human solidarity has to be an assured position, with the widest range of variation, without theological interventions. Human solidarity has been a victim of the negation of life as the "original sin", the inviolable Ten Commandments written by God, the sword as the key to heaven, disowning alterity as paganism or heathenism, violation of the natural order by disclaiming diversity under the banner of monocentrism, refutation of "many-splendored universality" through evangelisation or terrorism. Human Solidarity can become a reality only when artists of dogma are replaced by artists of thought, when light bathes the majestic paradigms of our deeper selves.

Human solidarity demands new structures of thought, faith, and nature, harmonizing in the beauty of life, in the immensity (*virāṭ*) of the cosmos that envelops us in its embrace of Divinity, and in the open natural spaces of the unknown. No shadows of dogmas, no imprisonment in the deadening certainty of Revelation, no suicidal verdicts donning lineaments of religion, no drowning the flow of time, no omnipotence of God that strangulates the flux of time, choice and *puṇya*.

II. Human Solidarity is possible only in Polycentrism

While the world follows multiplicity of religions, a new sense of respect and understanding of others will have to be developed. We will have to inhabit the spiritual universe as a continuing relationship between the 'inside' and the 'outside'. There is no 'inside' without an 'outside'. It has to be a developing realization in the dream-space of humans. Without diminution of religious autonomies, we will have to own the 'other'. Alterity or otherness with be integral to humanity. No universal mission for the management of the world, only the acceptance of pluralism as well as respect for multiplicity. We have to pass from de facto plurality to pluralism. It has to be an authentic human plenitude of various strands, held together by mutual respect. We have to avoid abstract and faceless principles. The thoughtless imposition of one universal validity can dehumanize. Humanity can function mainly on its intrinsic multiformity, by vindicating respect for each other. Without abolishing constitutive polarities, we can awaken the feeling of Human Solidarity in a pluralistic world. The deepest core of the humanum is in its bewildering intimacy of immensity and in the human values of divergence. In Webster's English Dictionary, the root word *civis* is akin to Sanskrit *Śiva*. Thus civilization rooted in the benign *Śiva* has to be a creative symbiosis to replenish humanity. It has to be away from the cold embrace of a universal cultural invariant.

The term higher religion hurts Human Solidarity. We have to evoke values of harmony, which can come front mutual respect, admiration of multiplicity, pantheism, and other like ideas and ideals. Universalism introduces hegemonic ideas. "Cultural commonality" cannot function as it will become skeletal without its flesh of variance. A uni-dimensional norm of humanity is against the deep reality of history. We have to discover freedom to acknowledge variousness. All the centuries, climes, lands, languages cannot be articulated according to a single symbol-system. The 'new science' is bringing in indeterminism, plural logical systems, quarks without substance, irrational numbers and so on. They compel us to a new sensibility of polycentric consciousness. Our century will have to be many-splendored, with a liveliness to sharing. It will not be a desire to control and manipulate societies through money or mind, sex or spirituality, power or privilege. No values exist in a vacuum. They have a history of centuries, exegeses of hundreds of minds, and the faith of millions. So concepts like 'cultural commonality' or 'universalism' will be counterproductive rather than creative. India has accepted and respected differences, the beauty of many forms, the eternality of various values. She has meshed the many in the harmony of divergence rather than of convergence. In the multi-

ple patterns of polycentrism alone can we find a meaningful movement
forward.

Respect for the cultures, civilizations and religions of each other, minus
conversions or interference by a subtle psychological agenda, alone should
be the values of humankind in our century.

Human Solidarity will be rich diversity, with no single meaning. The
various lines, the many realities will be lived in every one's deepest feelings. Cultures, in the plural, will be global in the sense that they will be
rooted in human consciousness as the vision and faith of Fellow beings,
whatsoever their demographic numbers. Universality of civilization, rather
than a universal civilization, will seek civil behaviour in the affirmation of
diversity. Such a civilization will be multiple and the centre will be everywhere.

Polycentrism emphasizes the principle of Many, and merges reality
with the secular world rather than with the sacral. It is a plurality of forces
functioning in life and nature. While monotheistic God has "unlimited authority", polycentrism is value, and multiplicity of perceptions at the highest levels of spiritual perfection. In 1935 Erik Peterson in his essay *Monothe-
ismus als politisches Problem* analyzed monotheism as a political problem.
French thinkers like Alain de Benoist seek a neo-pagan resurgence as a new
location of the sacred in plurality and freedom of human life. Polycentrism
is the bridge leading to Being immortal (*amṛtasyaiṣa setuḥ*) so that we live
and move and have its Joy (*ānanda*) in the consciousness of the Many of
the world.

III. The mind-ground of Human Solidarity can only be
Realization (*sādhanā*)

Revelation is the communication of God to human beings through a Prophet.
It is a condescension. It operates in three steps: (i) assertion, (ii) negation,
(iii) re-assertion:

(i) *assertion* in the scripture,
(ii) *negation* of those opposed,
   (Apostle Paul says: "They did not honour him as God ... Their sense-
   less minds were darkened" Rom. 1,21)
(iii) *re-assertion* in their suppression.

("The wrath of God is revealed from heaven against all ungodliness and wickedness of men" Rom. 1,18)

Revelation cannot be altered. It creates an Absolute, leads to a dogma, thence to violence and finally to terrorism. Human Solidarity can never begin.

Realization (*sādhanā*) is to visualize the harmony between man's spirit and the divine spirit of the universe, in the living growth of nature. It is a *rising* towards higher und nobler freedom of consciousness. In Realization or *Sādhanā* man ascends into a luminous vision of perfection, which in Revelation he accedes to imperatives. Realization is a caress of the heart to the inner sky of consciousness, to the *cidākāśa*. There are no pagans, no infidels in Realisation.

While in Revelation Man is in the image of God, in Realization gods are in the image of Man. Revelation is steeped in theism which "suggested that man's life an earth was significant only in so far as it affected his soul's expectation of God's mercy after death".

The Indo-European attitude of mind as revealed in Classical Greek und Roman writers attaches primary importance to man. The humanists of the Renaissance were against the belittling of human life and asserted its intrinsic value. The basic mind-ground of Realization (*Sādhanā*) is the greatness of human potentialities, the faring in the Grand of the universe. Realization is the ineffable serenity of Becoming, of which no predicate is possible.

As Revelation is the truth specially revealed in the history of a people nearest to God, it is both absolute and the kingdom of God is the eternal kingdom. It has given rise to the in mindset of the West that their kingdom is Absolute, and it is their imperative right to bring this 'one river of truth' to all. This monocentrism is the foundation of violence. Max Weber began his "Essays on the Sociology of Religion" with a statement of the uniqueness und universal importance of "Western" culture and civilization. The "inalienable rights and an indispensable moral responsibility" arising front the Revelation are responsible for human conflict instead of solidarity.

In natural homocentric cultures, time and place have a role to play. All becomes relative. Multiformity is part of the cosmic interplay of forces. Thus we have *yuga-dharma*, or the Buddhist concept of interdependent origination (*pratītya-samutpāda*). Humanity is itself the end, and not just a means.

IV. Human Solidarity and Transcendence

The Ten Commandments were spoken to Moses by God. Moses is the mouth-piece of God. The first commandment is an uncompromising prohibition of the worship of any deity other than God. The supremacy of God vis-à-vis man minimizes the importance of human life, and makes human beings the helpless play-beings of God. They have to wage crusades and its likes. In the paradigm of Transcendence, each Person is unique, who choses, thinks and contemplates. Existence rises into transcendence. Man becomes man-in-the-universe, "crossing the limiting barriers of the individual, to become more than man" (Tagore). Brahman of the Upaniṣads is the subtle reality of all things that exist, the very "beingness" of all beings, including human beings. It is the ennobling of man (*ud yānam te puruṣa*, RV), as contradistinguished from his compliance with Commandments. Transcendence is seeking, while the Commandments demand unquestioning submission. Processes of enlightenment are replaced by regimentation. The Vaiśeṣika-sūtra 1.1.2 defines Dharma as the attainment of the cosmic and a-cosmic *summum* (*yato 'bhyudaya-niḥśreyasa-siddhiḥ sa dharmaḥ*). It is man who comprehends the Divine and becomes Brahman. Man becomes immense in the highest abiding Joy (*Ānanda*). Life and the Divine are one. Existence and transcendence harmonize in wisdom. Man is responsible for his deeds or karma (*puṇyo vai puṇyena karmaṇā bhavati*, Bṛh 5.2.13). There is no word for the positive *puṇya* in Abrahamic religions, but only a word for the negative *pāpa* 'sin'.

V. Original Enlightenment versus Original Sin

A basic concept of Christianity is that the very fact of human birth is 'original sin'. Humans are born in sin. It is not so in Indic systems. The basic difference between Vedic and Abrahamic faiths is the concept of sin and virtue. Indic faiths do not have 'original sin'. Sin is an outcome of our actions, of our karma. Christianity has the word sin, but no specific word for *puṇya*, its positive aspect. In Indic systems, *pāpa* is sin, and *puṇya* is usually rendered as virtue, but virtue is *guṇa*.

Indic systems are rooted in agricultural concepts. The idea of karma stems from 'if we sow wheat we won't get rice, if we sow rice we won't get wheat'. Whatever we sow that is the harvest. Likewise, whatever actions a human being sows, they will be his harvest. Good deeds will bring good, and bad deeds will bring evil. Karma is that we are responsible for our deeds. The theory of karma affirms responsibility, and validates effort. The theory of reincarnation reinforces the primacy of good actions (*puṇya*). To cite the American poet Walt Whitman: "Not I, not anyone else can travel that road for you. You must travel it for yourself."

All living beings can attain enlightenment. It is a statement that all life is sacred and has innate enlightenment. Instead of 'original sin' of the Abrahamic tradition, it is the doctrine of 'Original Enlightenment' that respects life, and can become a solid base for Human Solidarity.

Frontiers create barriers in human understanding. An unchanging holy domain, rooted in the immutable word, in worldliness worked out in pain-staking detail in rigid theological structures, breeds a closed sacrum, which has to be defended with all one's might. Subject to the exigencies of power, it has to own aggressiveness and the vitality of violence.

Instead of frontiers, our century needs open horizons, where peoples are "sculptors of themselves", to invoke the light and lyricism that lives in our life. As the great poetess of Kashmir Lalleśvarī says: "from the outward enter into the most inward part of thy being".

VI. Diversity is the Law of Nature

Bio-diversity is the supreme law of nature. There are over a hundred thousand species of flora and fauna in India alone, more than a lakh of forms of plant and animal life in our country. Likewise, faith has to divine the several meanings of spiritual life, the fuzzy wisdom of nature, the light of the Many, and to image the sacrament that enshrines the Multiple, the Changing, the Silent. Let us not wound humanism with 'The Only True One'. The One has to become the Many. Theo-diversity is an inescapable corollary to the astounding discoveries in science und their universal application in technology. Theo-diversity alone will ensure the ascension of humanity to light and nobility that makes Joy (*sac-cid-ānanda*) not an attribute of the spirit, but its essential nature. Our century seeks a creative and imaginative reflection an the spiritual destiny of humankind, away from the disembodiment of the human at the altar of monocentric theism. Theo-diversity will lead us to the spontaneity of the fountains of the mind and make human sharing substantive.

Our century demands new structures of thought, spirituality, and nature harmonizing in the beauty of life, in the immensity (*virāṭ*) of the cosmos that envelops us in its embrace of Divinity, and in the open natural spaces of the unknown: No shadows of dogma, no imprisonment in
the deadening certainty of Revelation, no cutting down the venerable oak-
trees of centuries for bushes, no verdicts of suicidal decisions donning lineaments of religion, no drowning the flow of time, no omnipotence of God
that strangulates the flux of time, choice and *puṇya*.

VII. Path to Harmony

After millennia of separate histories, mankind now suddenly finds itself
in a common Situation. Natural resources dwindling, water table going
down every year, pollution reaching critical levels, social relationships being dominated by egotism, and national frontiers meaningless array: all
threaten human life itself. The technosphere is an a collision course against
the biosphere. Humanity needs a dynamic transformation. It has to be a
meaningful arrangement of different orders. It has to be a symbiosis of the
multiple, a polycentric consciousness.

The confluence of the nobility of several traditions, functioning in their
respective domains, can ensure a harmony of Life, Nature and Enlightenment (*Bodhi*) from the beyond within. Our self must be born anew every
moment in the rhythm and repose of the Spirit.

Human solidarity will emerge from a shared world, a world where differences are respected, where interdependence is the root of consciousness,
where monocentrism is abrogated, where the Absolute is subjected to an
ever-dynamic ascension to higher and higher absolutes in the plural and
in transition in all ages. No frozen or petrified dogmas posed as teleologies.

To end, a passage from the Buddhist Āgamas where tiny leaves am
hidden symbols, and in the symbols is the shade of panhuman values. In his
meditation Siddhārtha "looked up at a *pippala* leaf imprinted against the
blue sky, its tail blowing back and forth as if calling him. Looking deeply at
the leaf, he saw clearly the presence of the sun and stars. Without the sun,
without light and warmth, the leaf could not exist. He also saw in the leaf
the presence of clouds—without clouds there could be no rain, and without
rain the leaf could not be. He saw the earth, time, space, and mind—all
were present in the leaf. In fact, at that very moment, the entire universe

existed in that leaf. The reality of the leaf was a wondrous miracle." Just as the whole of life and nature are linked up in a seamless web, Human Solidarity is peace with nature, peace between humans, and peace within ourselves. Human Solidarity will drink her dreams from ecological peace, social peace and spiritual peace, in a where without a who.

11. Chapter

Can Compassion Foster Human Solidarity? A Christian Perspective

DIRK EVERS

IN MY PAPER, I want to deal with the subject whether and if so in which way compassion can foster human solidarity. I am going to unfold my subject in a succession of four theses. First of all I want to point to a few crucial elements desperately needed for the development of political human solidarity. Therefore my first thesis is: *Human solidarity must be rooted in an ethos and in values and cannot be reduced to formal regulations.*

It was the illusion in Western modern political theory that personal convictions and ethical values were seen as private matters which were irrelevant for the organisation of public and economic affairs. A striking example is the so called First Amendment to the North American constitution which guarantees the free exercise of religion, freedom of speech and other rights. But the fathers of the American constitution like Thomas Jefferson interpreted it in such a way as to strictly distinguish between private and public matters. Jefferson coined the phrase 'wall of separation' for such a division between the public political realm and the private moral and religious convictions of an individual (cf. Dreisbach 2002). As long as the public order is not disturbed, the private convictions of individuals are of no interest for the government. Or as Jefferson commented: 'it does me no injury for my neighbor to say that there are twenty gods, or no God. It neither picks my pocket nor breaks my leg' (Jefferson 1904: 221).

In his book *The Wealth of Nations* and in other writings, 18th century economist Adam Smith uttered the thesis that, in a free market, an individual pursuing his or her own self-interest will also promote the good of his or her community as a whole. If only each individual is allowed to tend towards maximizing his or her own revenue, the total revenue of society as a whole is fostered, because the laws of the market are such as to promote a common good which was not part of the individual's original intentions. An example from The Wealth of Nations illustrates the simplicity of the principle: "It is not from the benevolence of the butcher, the brewer or the baker, that we expect our dinner, but from their regard to their own self interest. We address ourselves, not to their humanity but to their self-love, and never talk to them of our own necessities but of their advantages."

Or to refer to another, but similar distinction, one can quote the German philosopher Immanuel Kant who strictly distinguished between what he called 'morality' and 'legality'. The state is only concerned with legality, when it sets up rules of commerce and public order, but it must strictly withdraw from any interference with morality, with ethical values or religious convictions. While the state has to regulate public life through public laws, it cannot rule the hearts of its citizens and must not interfere with religious or other belief systems. It can only allow and give the opportunity for self-determined religions of ethical communities: 'But woe to the legislator who wishes to establish through force a polity directed to ethical ends! For in so doing he would not merely achieve the very opposite of an ethical polity but also undermine his political state and make it insecure. The citizen of the political commonwealth remains therefore, so far as its legislative function is concerned, completely free to enter with his fellow-citizens into an ethical union in addition [to the political] or to remain in this kind of state of nature, as he may wish' (Kant 1960: 87s).

This tradition of reducing ethics to normative, but only formal regulations is vital until today. Although more critical theories have tried to question the leading role of economic relations, modern liberal theories still take it for granted that any political theory can only provide formal regulations of justice and fairness, but sees values and convictions as not obliging and in the end irrelevant matters of individual convictions. Thus the American philosopher John Rawls has developed a concept of justice as fairness which refrains from marking out a specific notion of justice. Rawls does not argue in favor of certain convictions concerning the nature of the person, the nature of human relationships, the goals of human existence, or any concept of ultimate goods and a good life. He raises no truth claims concerning anthropology, but tries to construe a strictly operational concept of justice that rests on the idea of society as a system of fair cooperation, and not on any substantial good. What forces us to develop justice as fairness is nothing but 'the common interest in public order and security' (Rawls 1971: 211). Another example is the German philosopher Jürgen Habermas, who like Rawls wanted to move away from the predominance of economic and administrative rationalization for the shaping of society, and thus designed a discursive theory of democracy, which is centred around the concept of a political community which can collectively define its political will and implement it as policy at the level of the legislative system. In his view a post-metaphysical liberal and pluralistic democracy is based on a public sphere as a place of purely rational independent debate.

There is no doubt that the separation of state and religion, the freedom of religious exercise and the guarantee of civil right independent of a person's race, colour, sex, language, religion, political or other opinion is an extremely important achievement of modern societies which must not be given up, which on the contrary must be promoted and must become an established reality for all societies. But on the other hand there are severe problems linked with this concept which have to be addressed. They are related to the fact that the wall of separation between the private and the public sphere is an illusion.

First of all, such a society which is based on purely rational rules and regulations never existed. Even our modern pluralistic societies are not value-free. There has always existed a hidden consensus which rests on notions of a good life and is grounded in human solidarity.

The most recent example that even economics is more than regulation is the financial crisis which reveals itself as a moral crisis of trust as well. It has taught us that formal rules and regulations are not enough. We need an ethos which is effective and obliging and which has the power to provide means and ends for human social life in pluralistic, multi-ethnical, multi-religious societies affected by global economics. Greed, lies, corruption and utopian speculations are part of this crisis, and they cannot only be countered by more and more effective formal regulations, but must also be met by a new sense of justice and solidarity. There is no economy without an element of trust. The notion that individual egoistic behaviour leads to a common good, is proven to be an illusion.

The total separation of the public and the private is an illusion. And this illusion can become dangerous because it promotes the notion that economical rationality is everything that counts. In a world which reduces human encounter and relationships to economic relations economical rationality imposes itself as the theory of everything. If the critical quest for integrity, truth and obligation is suspended, trends are fostered that present the supposedly self-evident economic necessities as the unquestionable foundations. The reduction of society to a functional sphere of mutual fairness reduces society to economics and the individual to a consumer. The meaningfulness of the good is replaced by the attractiveness of goods.

Thus I proceed to my second point asking: Why is that so? Where does the attractiveness of this model come from and why does it develop such a universal power in our times of globalisation?

My second thesis is, that *the attractiveness and the danger of a purely formal notion of society both lie in the fact that it does not deal with the ambiguities of human otherness.*

The other human being we experience both as a necessary condition for the development of our own individuality and as an obstacle and hindrance for it. It was one of the fundamental insights of 20th century existential philosophy that it identified the ambivalence, the tension between a human being and the other, between "I" and "Thou", as a central problem for the modern concept of personality and identity. The fact that human individuals always find themselves in the midst of others is not only a prerequisite for the development of an individual identity; it is also a source of constant pressure when others impose a certain view on us, while we strive for acknowledgment and recognition. Martin Heidegger pointed to this ambiguous character of the encounter with the other. Alongside our acquaintance with the material things around us we are also confronted with non-material entities, i.e., the others. At the same time Martin Buber distinguished between our "I-It"- and our "I-Thou"-relationships. Other human beings do not co-exist with us in the same sense as material things do. When we encounter other human beings, we always encounter them as inhabiting their own world and thus *existing* similar to us and not just being there. We file them not as things among things but as beings that have to project, to sketch out their existence according to their cares and concerns. Thus "the others" points to a category of ontological similarity:

We are not different from the others, we are among the others (cf. Heidegger 1986: 118). Therefore we do not relate to the others that co-exist with us as we do to material things – that is, not in a way of managing care (*Sorge* or *Besorgen*), but in a way of concern (*Fürsorge*, Heidegger 1986: 121).

This concern can be twofold. It can supply for the needs and concerns of the other and hence stand in for him (or as Heidegger says, "leaping in for the other" [*einspringen*]) and take over for the other what he should take care of himself. Concern for the other in this sense can, as Heidegger puts it, throw the other out of position by dominating the other and making him dependent. This is the way one "takes care of," for example, pets, children, the elderly, the sick and the injured. Therefore we have to distinguish between positive and negative interventions on behalf of the other—with the borderline between true solicitude respecting, even strengthening and fostering the other in his otherness, or dependency that deprives the other of his existential care and concerns by ways of paternalism.

But the other is not only the other individual. "The other" is also a trans-subjective category. All the others including myself form the common sphere of the public (*Öffentlichkeit*). I live my life as 'one' does life one's life. Most of the time, we exist in a levelled everyday mode of existence characterised by ordinariness. The others become the public, and the public provides the primordial interpretations of existence. Thus the concept of the others as the abstract public obscures and conceals existence as the task of being oneself by exculpating us from this task. Or as Heidegger put it: "Everyone is the Other and no one himself." [„Jeder ist der Andere und Keiner er selbst.“]

It is the signature, the task of modernity that we must always strive towards authenticity in which we can overcome the tension between individuality and commonality. In this tension we need the other in order to develop our individuality, and for the same reason we have to be different from the other, we have to reject the other in order to be just ourselves and not to lose our identity to the common sphere. Thus modern human beings in their relationships to others are constantly alternating between repulsion and attraction. Or as the French existentialist philosopher and writer Jean-Paul Sartre once wrote in his play *At closed doors*: "*L'enfer, c'est les autres*: Hell is other people."

In this situation modern liberal economy offers a model for dealing with this tension: If we reduce the public sphere to formal and basically economic regulations, then everyone can in his private existence develop his or her individuality. But freedom does not necessarily grow in proportion with the technological and economic means we develop, and while individual self-determination has become the central ideal of western culture, we are in danger to lose overall and obligatory aims and values which in turn are necessary for our public relationships.

Thus I come to my third point: How can we avoid this pitfall and nourish a notion of human solidarity which can balance between individuality and commonality and which can provide a solid ethical obligation for our public and political sphere? It is at this point where the notion of compassion comes in which is a universal feature of all major religions. Thus I assert my third thesis: *The notion of compassion is able to foster human solidarity. It is based on fundamental human character traits, but as an episodic emotion it is incomplete and ambivalent.*

In the history of Western thought it was by no means without controversy that compassion is a positive value with regard to morality and society. Though in the great epics and tragedies of the ancient Greek tradition like those of Homer, Aeschylus, Euripides, Sophocles suffering and sympathy were seen as natural human phenomena, the ancient philosophers started to questions their moral value. Our English term "compassion" and its equivalents are, by the way, directly derived from the Latin translations of the original Greek expressions. The terms under consideration are ἔλεος, οἶκτος, συμπάθεια, in Latin *commiseratio, compassio, misericordia,* in English *commiseration, compassion, pity.* Passion means suffering, while com-passion means co-suffering with the misery and pain of others (cf. the German term "Mitleid", established only in the 17th century as a translation of the Latin word in biblical texts). Compassion is seen as a spontaneous reaction to the suffering of others which usually results in spontaneous actions to mourn with the other, to comfort and to help him.

But already Plato argued against compassion in morality and pointed to the fact that only human beings suffer while the Gods are passionless. It is human to suffer when one loses something like wealth or health, but it is divine and rational to stand above emotional conflicts. Judges and political rulers must not decide according to their emotions but according to reason and justice. Thus Homer's epics and the tragedies are of no educational use, because they only present emotional movements and do refer to the necessary principles of rational regulation. This strand of argument was later taken over by the Stoics who rejected compassion as a positive virtue because it is not compatible with their ideals of independence and self-governing which required a total absence of passion.

Aristotle then was able to develop a different view. He understood compassion as a passion which becomes a virtue when it is controlled by reason. In his Rhetoric he formulated a first and influential definition which the history of Western thought referred to through the centuries. Aristotle writes: Compassion (ἔλεος) is "a kind of pain excited by the sight of evil, deadly or painful, which befalls one who does not deserve it; an evil which one might expect to come upon himself or one of his friends, and all that when it seems near" (Rhet. II,8,2). According to Aristotle compassion is a natural emotion because it is an example for the "the general principle that what we fear for ourselves excites our pity when it happens to others" (ibid.).

A few aspects of Aristotle's definition are of general interest. First of all compassion is a reaction towards real and dangerous evil (Aristotle speaks of an evil which is deadly or painful). Additionally compassion is triggered when three principles are fulfilled: the principle of "non deserving", of commonality and of proximity. With this definition in mind Aristotle can refer to positive functions of poetry and tragedies with regard to compassion: They transform passions (πάθος) including compassion into the ethical (ἔθος) by cultivating them according to their basic rational principles. Thus according to Aristotle compassion is an emotion which has to be refined and governed by reason.

It was this interpretation which the Christian tradition took over and elaborated. Now compassion became the positive motion of the heart which motivates human beings to see the misery of the other and to help one another. St. Augustine for example contrasts the Stoic ideal of emotionlessness with the Christian idea of love for the neighbour and he asks: "What is compassion but a fellow-feeling for another's misery, which prompts us to help him if we can? And this emotion is obedient to reason, when compassion is shown without violating right, as when the poor are relieved, or the penitent forgiven" (Augustine, City of God, IX, 5).

This was the predominant view throughout the middle ages, but in early modernity, when philosophy moved away from theological predominance, the dispute whether or not and under which circumstances compassion can be considered to be of positive ethical value. The Dutch philosopher Spinoza e.g. regarded compassion as useless, because as an emotion it weakens our moral power and adds nothing to the commandments of reason. The French materialists understood compassion mainly as an act of self-love, because it is triggered by the fear to possibly fall victim to the same evil which the pitied fellow human being suffers. It has no value in itself. Especially the German 19th century philosopher Friedrich Nietzsche regarded compassion as weakness, as directed against life, because life is founded on the will to power, whereas compassion was in his views invented by the unprivileged and deprived to counter that will. Compassion and pity are not only degrading the recipient but also the giver when they weaken his power to live. Thus Nietzsche warns against what he calls 'the conspiracy of the sufferers against the well-formed and victorious' (Nietzsche 1980: 864 [Zur Genealogie der Moral, III. 14]). Compassion is justified only as long as it derives from an overflow of strength, from an abundance of happiness, and not from an emotional identification with the weak and suffering thus contributing to the trends of degeneration propagated by Christianity and some moral philosophers (cf. Nietzsche 1980: 731).

But throughout the history of Western thought we also find the advocates of compassion until this very day. Let me just mention three from different traditions. In the English-Scottish tradition of common sense philosophy we find Adam Smith who in his *Theory of Moral Sentiments* proclaims compassion as "a fellow-feeling for the misery of others" which is a natural inclination induced "by changing places in fancy with the sufferer" (Smith 1976: 10). In 19th century German philosophy it was Arthur Schopenhauer who proclaimed compassion as the one authentic root of morality. He was inspired by Buddhist thought which in his understanding reveals the identity of all living beings. Therefore Schopenhauer understood the identification with the suffering of others as "practical mysticism" (Schopenhauer 1972: 273) in which one realises the unity of all beings. In the 20th century Th. W. Adorno recurred to Schopenhauer's notion of compassion and interpreted it as a necessary supplement to a purely rationalistic ethics. Compassion cannot be transformed into a theoretical notion, but it is a fundamental impulse of human solidarity with all suffering creatures. And thus Adorno explicitly includes animals as objects of human compassion. Only an ethics which is able to integrate compassion can overcome rationalistic excuses for exploitation and repression which are so characteristic for blind ideologies. That implies that compassion as the mere feeling of pity is not enough. It must turn into action and it must become aware of the reasons of human suffering. In its concentration on the concrete suffering, compassion as pity is always in the danger of ignoring structural evil. But on the other hand compassion is indispensible because it arises out of a sense of humanity and human dignity spontaneously identifies when human dignity is violated.

Let me summarize: Compassion is a natural, a universal, obliging and effective feature of any human being. It arises out of sense with which we develop empathy when we see ourselves in the places of others. It arouses a spontaneous feeling of human dignity when it indicates a situation of a fellow human being as impaired, as damaged, as a situation that should be different. This basic moral impulse of wishing for the well-being of other human beings is indispensible for any ethics. But, as the discussion through the centuries has made clear, compassion as an episodic emotion is incomplete and ambivalent. It cannot be transformed into a theoretical category, but it has to be developed into a virtue. It can lose its authenticity when it either becomes paternalistic or when it ignores structural conditions of evil by indulging in pity. Compassion in the right sense is a combination of both, nature and nurture.

With this result I come to my fourth and last thesis. *Compassion rests on a natural disposition, but because of its antagonists needs nurture and maturation it needs to be elaborated, to be taught, to be acquired and to be applied:*

a) Science can teach us about the natural mechanisms of empathy and basic social behaviour.

b) Religions offer means for the development of compassion by linking the spontaneous emotion to ultimate human concerns and concepts of the meaning of life.

Let me elaborate on this thesis a little further. Interestingly enough, modern science has proven that we are hard-wired for empathy. From the very beginning of our human existence, that is soon after birth we begin learning by imitating other human beings. Recent brain research has referred to so called mirror neurons, a certain type of neuronal cells which fire both when an animal acts and when the animal observes the same action performed by another (especially conspecific) animal. In that way certain parts of the brain mirror the behaviour of another animal, as though the observer were executing the action itself. These neurons have been directly observed in primates, and are believed to exist in humans as well. These structures explain why newborn infants (of primates as well as of humans) are immediately able to imitate facial expressions of adults.

Human babies soon know how to detect the direction of intentional behaviour of adults and instinctively distinguish between living beings and inanimate objects and between intentional and non-intentional actions. They have mechanisms of gaze-following, and when they grow older they try to verify the attention of adults in critical situations. With the age of 13 to 15 months they develop gestures to direct the attention of adults in order to share observations with them – a feature not known in the animal kingdom. Thus even before they can speak, children acquire a repertoire of what scientists have called declarative gestures, with which they can share attention and intentional behaviour with others.

The next step is reached when children go from participating in shared intentionality to participating in collective intentionality (cf. Tomasello and Rakoczy 2003). They begin to make friends with others; they develop a sense of being a family member and how to follow rules and norms. All this is accompanied by the development of basic notions of fairness and justice which stabilise social interactions.

Interestingly enough, recent research has found out that the traditional standard theory of economics had started with wrong presuppositions. "Traditional models of economic decision-making assume that people are self-interested rational maximisers who try to get as much out of a situation as possible. Empirical research has demonstrated, however, that people will take into account the interests of others and are sensitive to norms of cooperation and fairness. In one of the most robust tests of this finding, the ultimatum game, individuals will reject a proposed division of a monetary windfall [Zufall], at a cost to themselves, if they perceive it as unfair" (Jensen, Call and Tomasello 2007: 109). Recently it had been shown that in such an ultimatum game chimpanzees indeed are rational maximizers and are not sensitive to fairness. "These results support the hypothesis that other-regarding preferences and aversion to inequitable outcomes, which play key roles in human social organization, distinguish us from our closest living relatives" (ibid.).

As one of the key features which enable us to develop as social beings, cognitive science has identified a specific cognitive ability of human beings which it calls Theory of Mind. That is the ability to understand others as intentional agents and to interpret their minds in terms of theoretical concepts of intentional states such as *beliefs* and *desires*. Between 3 and 5 years of age children learn how to take beliefs and desires of other human beings into consideration for their own actions. In this way, they develop a sense of what it means to be a human being among human beings. This also puts certain Darwinian concepts into perspective which see competition, survival of the fittest and the struggle for existence as the main features of evolution. The new insights mentioned point to the fact that we are basically social beings, and that our motivational systems are directed towards empathy, cooperation and relationship building.

But all these abilities which human beings acquire and develop are only the necessary prerequisites for compassion, they are not sufficient for it, because they cannot overcome the ambivalences between human beings. Human compassion and solidarity is on the one hand deeply grounded in basic human properties such as empathy and instinctive pity for the needy. On the other hand it suffers from the ambivalence of human relationships, the tension between Ego and Alter, between myself and the other. Mere pity focuses only on the conditions of suffering and even widens the gap of distance, of separation, of otherness between the pitying agent and the pitied person. Authentic Compassion, by contrast, develops attentive concern for the suffering person, is based on awareness of our common humanity and thus, at its best, is able to bridge the damaging gap of separation and otherness with its associated negative feelings.

My suggestion is to rediscover religions as resources for promoting and educating compassion as a basis for human solidarity. All religions offer concepts and tools for a cultivation of compassion as a virtue. Although religions too often have been part and parcel of divisions between human beings by the exclusion of others, by religious justifications of differences, they also in their core beliefs have developed means of overcoming differences on the grounds of ultimate concerns and have provided effective motivation for turning towards the needy and the suffering. They have tried to balance self-identity and selflessness on the grounds of a common human identity. And they have tried to reconcile the difference between a person and the other by seeing the other as a representation of the divine.

Religions have usually done this by presenting role models, narratives and character forming ritual practices. They do not only refer to theoretical concepts of otherness and compassion, because they know that compassion in its authentic form is not a rational theory, but an integration of both ultimate concerns and emotional dispositions. Religions do not only communicate information and intellectual skills, they also communicate the spirit of being human. They keep alert our sense of that which cannot be calculated, but is beyond profit and interest. And we now know: even our common economical market needs the incalculable for the calculations to work. By presenting role-models from the past like the Good Samaritan or the Buddha religions present possible options which are not theoretical concepts but offer the chance to act similarly and in that way to practice the shift from mere pity to active mercy without losing, but by actively realising one's own identity.

Thus religions seem to promote compassion vertically and horizontally. Vertically they frame compassion as the *imitation* of a role model, of Jesus, the prophet, the Buddha, of God himself in his ultimate mercy. Horizontally they provide foundations and means for *identification* between human beings (e.g. as children of God or the Divine). Different concepts of compassion might be compared along these lines.

Insofar as religions see the foundation of compassion in the divine which is not within the reach of human action, they also point to *limits of compassion.* Unlimited compassion might turn into terror for both, for the subject as well as for the object of compassion. It can lead to feelings of superiority and contempt on the part of the pitying individual and to feelings of alienation, shame, and inferiority on the part of the pitied. Conceptualising compassion within a comprehensive framework of God himself being merciful is a means against both, feelings of superiority and inferiority.

For the final conclusions let me once again return to the beginning of my presentation. I had started with the thesis that our political and economic culture needs more than formal regulations, but is deeply dependent on universal, obliging and effective grounds of human solidarity. I then tried to show you that there is a biological basis for empathy and compassion, but that it is not sufficient to overcome the ambivalences which exist between human beings. Compassion and solidarity need to be nurtured, developed and educated and religions provide concepts and tools for doing so by linking our natural dispositions to ultimate concerns.

In our secular, pluralistic and multi-religious societies which are embedded into an emerging global economy the dissolution of the knowledge, the practice and the obligatory character of religious traditions poses a challenge. Religious institutions and organisations have once and for all lost their monopoly. The modern pluralistic state cannot provide ultimate orientation, but is at the same time dependent on resources which it can neither produce nor guarantee (Böckenförde 1967: 93). Therefore we need new forms of public discourse on moral value in which religious and secular institutions work together. The reduction of religion to a matter of private opinion is no longer appropriate.

What we urgently need are conventions like this in which interreligious dialogue does not primarily deal with doctrinal matters, but where a fruitful exchange of practical concepts is exercised by which we can learn from one another, question one another and develop a critical and thus deeper understanding of the obligations we feel towards our own tradition. And at the same time we might provide common insights, motivations and relevant role-models for our societies in the global context. We need public arenas where the implications of religious and non religious world-views and moral concerns can be openly discussed, questioned and responsibly defended. In such places the legitimacy, truth and validity for such convictions should be respectfully, but critically discussed and investigated, not only by outsiders who speak about their subject, but by representatives who are actively involved in the development of their respective tradition. I think that it is not an unwarranted expectation to anticipate that such discussions, where the wall of separation between the private and the public becomes penetrable, will not only have a cleansing and educational effect for the respective religious traditions, but will also do good for society as a whole.

References

Böckenförde, E.-W., 1967: Die Entstehung des Staates als Vorgang der Säkularisation, in: *Säkularisation und Utopie*, Stuttgart, 75–95.

Jensen, K., J. Call, and M. Tomasello, 2007: Chimpanzees are rational maximizers in an ultimatum game, *Science* 318(5847), 107–109.

Nietzsche, F., 1980: *Werke in drei Bänden*, Vol. II, K. Schlechta (ed), Munich.

Schopenhauer, A., 1972: Preisschrift über die Grundlagen der Moral (1841), in: A. Hübscher (ed), *Werke*, Vol. IV, third edition, Frankfurt a.M.

Smith, A., 1976: *The theory of moral sentiments* (1759), D. D. Raphael and
   A. L. Macfie (eds), Oxford.
Tomasello, M. and H. Rakoczy, 2003: What Makes Human Cognition Uni-
   que? From Individual to Shared to Collective Intenionality, *Mind &
   Language* 18/2, 121–147.

12. Chapter

Compassion and solidarity in international relations

Roberto Toscano

IN A WORLD CHARACTERIZED not only by cruel conflicts, but also by an often violent rediscovery of ethnic identities it seems utopian and naive even to suggest that relations between human groups and between nation states can factor in considerations and policies inspired by human compassion and solidarity. Both the extremist ideologues of warring fundamentalisms and self-styled realist theoreticians - in reality mere ideologues, and often of an extremist kind - invite us to take stock of the irreconcilable nature of hostilities and clashes of material interest and cultural and religious orientations. Solidarity, and in general ethics, should be confined, they maintain, to the realm pious religious meekness or philosophical abstraction.

In international relations, the followers of the realist school (by and large the dominating school, especially among professionals in the field) have traditionally been allergic to ethical issues, postulating instead the functioning of a system composed of intrinsically amoral subjects (nation-states) engaged in the disembodied pursuit of rational goals. What is singular is that this apparently Machiavellian approach eludes the explicitly ethical focus of Machiavelli's entire theoretical construction, a focus that has been analyzed with definitive clarity by Isaiah Berlin.

Realists in international relations, in other words, have the tendency to hide their own ethical preference in favor of the nation-state (their own brand of partial ethics) under a supposedly neutral "extraethical" cover.

The time has come to challenge this view and show, instead, that compassion and solidarity are not only as real a component of human beings as violence, but that they are an imperative, and not an option, if we want to avoid devastating and permanent conflict.

International relations cannot be made ethics-free, neither in theory nor in practice. In the first place, even the most radical defenders of national interest in theory and practice (i.e. not only American neocons, but also traditional conservatives) couch their international behavior in moral terms: the enemy is not only an opponent or contender in terms of power or resources, but is evil.

Secondly, the power of nation-states is not only military or economic, but is also hegemony (Gramsci) or "soft power" (Nye), i.e. is based on the capacity not only to impose, but to convince.

Having said that even "realists" are obliged to deal with an ethical discourse, it is important to see why an ethical discourse is, by itself of no guarantee of compassion and solidarity.

The key aspect here is the mechanism of inclusion/exclusion. Apart from sociopaths (those that positivist XIX century criminologists defined as affected by "moral madness") no individual lives without accepting a circle within which he recognizes the duty ton take into account the rights of other individuals as well as solidarity towards them. Family, clan, nation, race, religion, political party or at times even a soccer club or a criminal gang mark the perimeters within which not only material obligations, but also moral duties, are accepted and abided by.

The problem arises when one of these circles, any of them, is taken as the only relevant one. When only one identity, that is (be it national, religious, party) is taken as a final moral perimeter. Thus we see individuals who are angels in the family and devils outside ("amoral familism"), others who are pious and compassionate within their religious community and kill "infidels" with no qualms, others who are inspired by lofty humanist goals but decree with nonchalance the elimination of the "class enemy", others who are sensitive to culture and spirituality and can run an extermination camp for an "inferior race".

In this post-Cold War, beginning-of-the-Millennium disorienting and disoriented historical phase it is fashionable to talk about the irrepressible urge of groups – having not only to cope with the destructuring of the previous international system, but also the disturbing prospects of globalization - to find solace and reassurance in a strengthened identity as a prerequisite not only of psychic health but also of survival itself and of

effective common action. At the same time, not so long ago we have witnessed the horrors perpetrated by the violent pursuers of identity, from
ethnic cleansing in former Yugoslavia to genocide in Rwanda while other
such horrors are looming in many parts of the world. What are we then
to think, in both political and ethical terms, about identity? Is it bad or
"good"? Or perhaps – as many nationalists will tell you – are we just facing excesses, exaggerations (practiced by people who are for one reason or
the other "savage") in something that is essentially good?

Actually the problem is not a quantitative, but a qualitative one. Not
all identity is conflict generating. On the contrary, identity is the prerequisite even of altruism and love and, in group terms, of all kinds of positive
interaction in terms of exchange and solidarity What is conflict generating is not identity per se, it is what can be called "narcissistic identity" the
kind of identity whose affirmation, pursuit, and defense form an integral
part of the essence of nationalism (and of its lesser but not less potentially
murderous counterparts, communalism and tribalism).

Why is this so? In the first place, because at the root of group identity lies …a lie, or – put in less blunt terms – a cultural artifact, an intellectual construct produced by elites that have been very aptly defined by
Pierre Bourdieu "as professional producers of subjective visions of the social world". It is commonly believed (especially by nondemocratic political
leaders) that in order to maintain the cohesion of a group it is not enough to
define its identity in objective terms: all those born on the same territory,
all those sharing the same religion, all those speaking the same language.
To be fair, finding objective criteria for group identity is indeed problematic. If we go hunting for what have been defined as "crucial markers of
identity" and take for instance language, we see that on that basis no identity of post-Yugoslav entities would have been possible, since they all spoke
Serbo-Croatian. The same is true in the case of Rwandan Tutsis and Hutus,
all speaking the same language: in this case, not even the "crucial marker"
of religion would work, since both Hutus and Tutsis are mainly Catholic.
More than hypothetical racial differences, or no longer intact social ones,
often the deadly "crucial marker" – as in the case of the 1994 genocide of
Tutsis - ends up being the most bureaucratic of all artifacts: a mention of
ethnicity on identity cards. For this reason, there must be what has been
called "the invention of tradition", there must be the creation of "imagined
communities", there has to be a "founding myth". The group must have

in all cases noble, ancient origins (divine, if possible); it must bask in the past glories of invincible ancestors or it must brood over the historical injustice visited upon it by a military defeat or an alien invasion depriving it of previous power and well-being. The point is that such an artificial, ideological path to identity is inherently conflict generating: in the first place, because by abandoning factual, falsifiable criteria it opens the door to controversy that has no possible solution but force; in the second place, because myths are by definition not objects of possible compromise, especially when your neighbors hold about the same territory and the same history incompatible myths of their own; in the third place, because the positive self-stereotyping that is an essential component of this narcissistic identity inevitably requires a negative stereotyping of the Other, of the neighbor. But, most of all, because narcissist group identity, by making one's own group's value incomparably higher qualitatively incommensurable with that of any other group, ends up denying the ethical relevance of the Other, i.e., expels the other from the scope of applicability of moral rules. Thus, when real or perceived conflicts of interests, real or perceived threats originate from another group, the human individual, who as a rule, as the Romans said, *abhorret a sanguine* (refrains from blood), reacts together with the group in ways that are totally detached from the ethical standards that her or she would uphold as an individual without seeing, as a rule, any contradiction between being "a good person" and a ferocious soldier for the group (be it the nation state or the tribe).

The theme of human solidarity, and of its importance as a dimension of international relations, is a very vast one, and it would be overly ambitious to try to embrace its full scope in the limited space of a short talk. I will instead limit myself to examining three aspects of the question that I believe deserve our attention.

I. Are Compassion and Solidarity "Un-natural"?

Self-styled realists, both in the held of anthropology/sociology and in that of international relations, try to convince us that human nature is basically aggressive, and that compassion and solidarity are the artificial and superficial products of moral indoctrination, a precarious and thin layer that is cast off as soon as real interests and real passions take over. In this we find the traces of a superficial interpretation of Darwinism, with its vulgar version of "the survival of the fittest". In reality instead of scientific Darwinism what is at play here is *social* Darwinism, a XIX century ideological construct in which there is more Spencer than Darwin.

It is interesting here to quote Adam Smith, a thinker that is considered one of the founders of individualist, free-enterprise liberalism. In his book *The Theory of Moral Sentiments* he wrote: "How selfish soever man may be supposed, there are evidently some principles in his nature which interest him in the future of others, and render their happiness necessary to him, though he derives nothing from it except the pleasure of seeing it."[1].

True science tells us something completely different from the pseudo realism of *homo homini lupus*, i.e. that solidarity and compassion are as "natural" as violence, and that, indeed, the individual without compassion is the most unnatural of human beings, a sociopath.

Com-passion, sym-pathy mean sharing the other's pain, mean recognizing the other's common humanity and affinity. It means, quoting Emmanuel Levinas, recognizing the face of the Other.

This is so true that those who want to promote the killing of the enemy engage in a systematic action aiming at erasing the concrete face of the Other: "We have a natural inclination not to kill our own kind, and therefore we have to make them horribly unlike us before we can overcome our instinctual compassion and kill them"[2]. I am convinced that ethics is supported not only by psychology and anthropology, but also by advanced biology. Isn't advanced biology, with its discovery of "mirror cells" telling us exactly the same thing on empathy? Thus, before culture there is also nature to prove that solidarity is not an artificial construct, an ideological preference, if not the product of wishful thinking.

Coexistence of different groups is indeed problematic and fragile, but at the root of violent group conflict (not simple tensions, not simple divergences, not simple controversies) we almost inevitably find the conscious, systematic, intellectually dishonest endeavor of political leaders aimed at convincing the group of: (a) its own uniqueness and nobility, (b) the despicable, treacherous nature of the rival group, stereotyped in abstract terms

---

[1] Quoted in Alfie Kohn, *The Brighter Side of Human Nature*, Basic Books, New York 1990, p. 44.

[2] Sam Keen, *Faces of the Enemy. Reflections on the Hostile Imagination* also quoted in the Kohn book, p. 48.

that leave no space for individual difference and exception; (c) the objective nature of certain group interests defined as unavoidable goals combined with the denial that there are always choices and that they are also determined by subjective values and not only by objective interests; and (d) the absolutely "zero-sum" nature of the rivalry often to the point of mutually exclusive survival (*mors tua, vita mea*). According to such terrorist technique, all issues (the use of a name or a flag, a few square miles of territory, the bank of a river or the top of a mountain) are presented as "vital" to the very survival of the group. To use Thomas Nagel's simile, "the last eclair on the dessert tray" is always described, in nationalist propaganda, as "the last life jacket for your own child".

With this last point we reach a very crucial aspect of the ethical discourse the incompatibility of ethics – any ethics – with the absolutization of a primordial striving for survival, what Spinoza calls *conatus essendi.*

Here we are not just facing a variant of possible ethical options but something much more radical. In fact, whereas ethics is by definition exclusively human, *conatus essendi* (i.e., the striving for the preservation of being) is, according to Spinoza a property of "things" in general, i.e. a naturalistic law on a par with the laws of thermodynamics. Thus, when it becomes the only or the absolutely overwhelming guiding principle for action (both individual and group) we are in a dimension where only causality reigns. Actions may not be traced back to the subject accomplishing them by the process of "imputation", the necessary connection to responsibility. This evidently makes all ethics - and also legality – inconceivable.

The tension between causality and agency, or imputation (i.e., between necessity and freedom) is another essential element for the definition of the field of ethics. One could say that, just as in the pre-modern world even causation of natural events tends to be interpreted in terms of imputation, of human responsibility (magic and witchcraft), in the postmodern world human action tends to be "naturalized" and read in terms of causality. In the former instance the ethical discourse is distorted by hallucination, absurdity, and arbitrary assignation of guilt; in the latter, the universalization of causality to cover human action means the end of responsibility, in other words, of the very-possibility of ethics. Only a never-resolved tension between causality (creating the framework, the limits and the conditioning of human action) and imputation (allowing the attribution of responsibility) can leave space for a complex ethical discourse in which causality justifies compassion, but imputation legitimizes judgment.

Opting for an ethical approach means, in essence, opting for Humanity against mere Being. Emmanuel Levinas states this point with great clarity:

> "Ontology – that is, the intelligibility of being – only becomes possible when ethics, the origin of all meaning, is taken as the starting point. Humanity must irrupt into Being: behind the perseverance, in being, of the beings or worlds – of men, too, insofar as they are themselves simple worlds – behind their *conatus essendi* or their identity, affirming its own ego or egoism, there must figure, somewhere, in some form or other, the responsibility of *the one for the others*."[3]

Having said that ethics (ethics that inhibits the recourse to group violence) requires cognizing and recognizing the face of the Other, making the Other concrete and not abstract – we should be very much aware of the fact that there are some faces we will never see. The problem of the use of group violence, in other words, is not only limited to the violence used literally against the neighbor, but also the violence visited upon distant peoples by our own group.

How do we deal with the anonymous, distant other? The ethical premise of our refraining from using or condoning violence can remain the same. Yet it will not take us far enough, and risks establishing a perverse proportionality between the geographical and cultural remoteness of a specific Other, the possibility to really *regarder son visage* and the degree of applicability of ethical standards (colonial violence was a clear example of this proportionality.)

For an orientation in the solution of this problem we can find interesting guidance in Levinas:

> "Indeed, if there were only two of us in the world, I and one other, there would be no problem. The other would be completely my responsibility. But in the real world there are many others. When others enter, each of them external to myself, problems arise. Who is closest to me? Who is the Other? Perhaps something has already occurred between them. We must investigate carefully Legal justice is required. There is need for a state."[4]

Thus the relevant pronouns are not only "I" and "Thou," but also "They". For a complete ethical cosmos, one needs to start from preservation and

---

[3] "Priere sans demande", *Etudes philosophiques*, 38, 1984, p.157.

[4] "Ideology and Idealism", in S. Hand, ed., *The Levinas Reader*, Blackwell, Cambridge, MA, 1989, p. 247.

the freedom of the Self (an essential prerequisite of all moral action), but then move on to a respect of the "Thou" based on recognition and leading to solidarity. But there is a third component, "Them", those who are inevitably third parties. Since they do not concretely come into contact with us, we have to apply rules, we have to be guided by justice. All law, including international law, belongs to this level.

What is important is that these three levels be constantly interconnected. Let us reflect, to prove this point, on the possible consequences of their disconnectedness., What is freedom of the Self without respect of the Other or justice? It is very significant, here, to see that the most radical defenders of extreme, nihilistic individualism – from Nietzsche to Bataille – utilize a term that is characteristic of the discourse on international affairs: *sovereignty*. Like the sovereign state, the sovereign individual is self-referential even in the realm of ethics. Like the sovereign state, the sovereign individual claims the right to kill in order to pursue specific ends.

But what is the recognition of the Other without justice? Here we have to go back to the essential concept of impartiality. The Other that cannot be the object of a direct relationship, that cannot be "individualized," risks being relegated to the outskirts of moral responsibility. Risks being treated unfairly vis-à-vis the more immediate, more concrete Other. Only justice can be a sort of moral safety net allowing for the inevitable limitations of concrete experience, for the objective difficulties we encounter in the search for the face of the Other.

But, also: what is justice without the freedom of the "I", if not ethically precarious submission to rulers? And what is it without the concrete "Thou"? Justice without solidarity, and without compassion, turns into the opposite of ethics. Since the writing and the application of the rule require a system, specifically a nation-state, then abstract justice, the abstract rule, can be (has been, historically) the path leading to violence against those who are "outside the rule." If not checked, relativized by the "I" and the "Thou," the rule embodied in the state is indeed one of the mainsprings of group violence: violence that is abolished internally by the application of the rule and that is discharged externally, since the applicability of the rule (and of the justice that the rule is supposed to apply) is only valid within the legal system that is, to the state. In this respect it would be of course absolutely absurd to maintain that German philosophy and political science (from Hegel to Schmitt, i.e., from the absolutization of the state to the centrality of the friend/enemy dichotomy) "produced" the Nazi phenomenon: but we can say that that philosophy and that political science were fully compatible with it.

II. Solidarity and rights

It is very important to clarify a necessary distinction between solidarity and rights. There is the danger, as a matter of fact, that proponents of a compassionate view of human relations (including international relations) will focus their discourse only on the moral quality of our behavior towards others, considering that behavior as noble but optional, and the product of free individual choice.

Solidarity, on the contrary, should be conceived as the moving force behind norms and institutions that give structure and content to human society. The international discourse on human rights is very clear on this point. Rights mean entitlement, duty of recognition, mechanisms of implementation.

This is why when we talk of human rights the objection voiced by so called realists on the basis of a relativist approach to moral principles is totally irrelevant. Solidarity and compassion identify a moral issue, usually thanks to the passion and commitment of individuals who are ahead of their time, and are considered dreamers or radicals. One example will suffice: slavery. A millenarian institution, practiced in all cultures and condoned by all religions (usually in glaring contradiction with their basic tenets) was first challenged by isolated, visionary individuals on the basis of human compassion, but later it turned into norms, both national and international.

Abolitionism was a minority moral cause before becoming a universal norm. The same can be said, though we are still in a transitional stage, about the extension of the concept and norms of human rights from civil and political rights only to embrace socio-economic and cultural rights.

Compassion tells us that it is not very consistent to maintain that there is a right to publish a dissident newspaper but not the right to feed your family. The Italian Constitution, in its article 36, says: "Workers have the right to a salary which is proportionate to the quantity and quality of their work, and in any case sufficient to guarantee to them and to their fami-

lies a free and dignified existence". It is interesting, though the actual en-
forcement of the rule is of course problematic, that there have been some
judicial decisions on the matter in cases of glaring "disproportion" and of
gross "insufficiency" of retributions. As both jurists and political scientists
agree, we are still very far from turning the whole range of socio-economic
and cultural rights into enforceable norms. Yet, we are clearly no longer
within the confines of mere human solidarity, without the possibility of
referring to rights and formulating claims.

III. Victimhood and Compassion

Recognizing the plight of the victim is central to setting in motion the
process that from compassion to active solidarity can bring about human
action – and can create a more humane system of norms and institutions.
Victimhood, on the other hand, is a concept that has to be handled with
care. The recognition of the status of victim has turned into a proliferation
of claims to victimhood, and often to reparations, that is rife with controversy and sometimes entails insoluble political problems.

The central difficulty in a sort of universal competition for recognized
victimhood is that victims of historical wrongs and horrors tend first, to
pretend to be a sort of "ontological victims" independently from present-
day action and circumstances and, second, they tend to be deaf to the often
equally justified claim to victimhood of others.

Granting ourselves the status of victims tends to go together with a
justificatory mechanism allowing us, *qua* victims, to exert violence – including the most horrendous, the most lawless and inhumane - on those
whom we identify as victimizers. Unscrupulous and militaristic leaders are
usually very skillful in playing the victim game.

The rationale of terrorist action, as can be clearly seen by reading the
statements of the authors of terrorist acts, almost inevitably includes the
claim of victimhood. The same can be said of torture, recently linked to the
claim of being victims of terrorism. Even in the case of genocide victimhood has played a role. Rwandan Hutus, the collective perpetrators of the
1994 genocide, were seeing themselves as the victims of century-old feudal
exploitation by the Tutsis as well as the imminent victims of an impending
genocide launched by them.

Historical wrongs and horrors should not be covered by denial, but the recognition of victimhood should be mutual and, especially, not considered a blanket authorization for illegal and immoral action.

To conclude, human compassion, the foundation of active solidarity, is not only ethically, but also psychologically, anthropologically and even biologically grounded. Not as an inevitable and invariable trait of humanity, since it can be overruled by passion or ideology (as well as by psychic disorder). Yet it is at least as real as the possibility of hostility and violence. This is also true in international relations, since the global dimension of human civilization is rendering less and less credible and sustainable the ancient drawing of limited circles of human recognition and ethical inclusion, and since the objective interconnectedness of human destiny on a global scale (from economic crises to environmental disasters, from terrorism to pandemic diseases) is pointing toward the need to extend our compassion and solidarity, thus our capacity to work together for survival and growth, from a restricted circle - the family, the tribe, our party, our race, our religious community - to humanity as such.

Not only a moral imperative, but an objective, "realist" need.

13. Chapter

Human Solidarity – A Diplomat's View

GIORGIO GIACOMELLI

IN HER WISDOM, our kind hostess has accurately composed this panel for a subject that, in its amplitude and complexity, requires to be tackled by many different points of view: philosophical, political, economical, humanitarian etc. But in addition, and upstream, it needs to be tackled from two basic approaches: The theoretical/academic one, in order to identify the appropriate way to follow and the correct definitions, and the empirical/pragmatic one, based on field experience, in order to identify its operational complexities and the many obstacles that one must expect to meet in this endeavor.

For sure the participants in this conversation are not one-track-minded, but each and everyone, on the basis of his inclination and his experiences, will tend to privilege one of these two approaches.

I mentioned all this, in order to introduce myself as belonging to the second category, may be to a certain extent for predisposition, but, above all, because of the experiences I have lived both as a diplomat and as a multilateral official.

En passant, I will remark that these two approaches cannot but favor, respectively, a more optimistic vision the first, and a more pessimistic the second. And that consequently the most promising approach is probably provided by an appropriate mix of the two.

To facilitate the identification of the most adequate methodology apt to foster a progressive globalization – to use a word in fashion – of human solidarity, I believe it is important to try and understand its very nature also from the anthropological point of view. To that end, we must consider that, notoriously, two basic parts of our brain are devoted to two fundamental functions: those related to the domain of instincts and emotions the first, and those concerning rationality, the second.

Now, while the first (for reasons beyond the scope of our conversation) has evolved at the pace of millions of years, the second has undergone an evolution that, in biological terms, can be defined as flashing (thousands of years!)

Consequence of this peculiarity is that in every man and every woman coexist two distinct personalities in perpetual conflict: one dominated by the primeval instincts and the other by reason.

Human solidarity is not exempt by this double track of human nature and therefore, originated as a means of defense and survival within the original small groups of hunters /gatherers, trudges to keep up with the present swift socio-cultural evolution of our species and to apply to its exponentially growing new size.

Result of this inconsequence is that, to the awareness of the necessity of adjusting human behavior to the new size, structure and organization of contemporary human society, does not correspond the capability to keep under control imperatives so deeply rooted in our nature.

If such combination of inclinations can, may be, contribute to make life more exiting, it is obvious that it exposes us to serious dangers insofar it makes the behavior of each and every human being – including that of the most powerful leaders, even those in control of deadly weapons of mass destruction – somehow erratic and unpredictable.

Truly, some progress has been made, both at the cultural and legislative level, often thanks to the vision, dedication and tenacity of some individuals that, throughout history, have endeavored to open the eyes and minds of their contemporaries, (often paying very dearly for it); but these are still exceptions. Therefore, as it is most unlikely that the human, ancestral nature can be modified in useful time, it is necessary to devise mechanisms apt to defuse the most dangerous consequences of it, keeping in mind that, combined with the new science and technology, they could easily lead to the extinction of our species.

Thus the urgent need to try and overcome this peculiarity of man gradually making him to understand and accept his appurtenance to a global community and thus the necessity of accepting some basic, cogent rules of behavior meant at imposing human solidarity beyond its traditional, poky borders.

In dealing with human solidarity it is necessary to distinguish its two main aspects: the solidarity between states – which refers mainly to peace keeping – and solidarity between people.

Aspects that, in spite of their obvious analogies and connections, present a macroscopic difference insofar the second can rely on cogent means of prevention and coercion meant to safeguard law and order, while the first disposes of very weak ones.

This weakness is, no doubt, at the origin of the efforts undertaken, especially in more recent times, to create international institutions delegated to foster and, when necessary, impose solidarity. Obviously it is not per chance that the more ambitious and structured of these initiatives have been taken in the aftermath of especially calamitous international conflicts.

Such tendency has given its most ambitious fruit at the conclusion of the Second World War with the creation of the United Nations, political organization *par excellence* that, together with an ever expanding set of specialized agencies, has given life to the United Nations System.

System complex and slow, especially because the decisional processes established in their charters have been adopted by member states under the influence of mental reservations, due to their obsession with safeguarding their egotistic interests. In the first place invoking the principle of sovereignty. As matter of fact this principle, originally meant to safeguard the independence and integrity of states, has become in our time the main obstacle to multinationality and the major excuse to avoid any real delegation of the power to impose the respect of the law. The records of the supreme political organ of the United Nations, the Security Council, provide ample evidence of such a tendency.

In conclusion we can assume that the main obstacle to progress in international solidarity derives from the reluctance of governments and political leaders to renounce to any significant part of their privileges and power.

Obviously this is a situation in which the beneficial potential of the System tends to be befogged by its cumbersomeness and the mental reservations that characterize it, combined with the incumbent effects of an imbalanced globalization.

To this respect it has to be noted that the complexity of the System is accentuated by the gradual intervention in the game of new protagonists, and in the first place by: the civil society – more and more autonomously organized and transnational –; the local governments; and the multinational companies. While the role of the first is of old, well meaning engagement, the others seem to have open only recently to the awareness and assumption of the enormous responsibility they also are facing.

Complexity, but may be also precondition and hope of its eventual success, in so far involving the main components of our society.

The hope of succeeding in building a more solidary world at the international level, seems therefore to lie in a – I am afraid arduous to obtain – less selfish and more responsible attitude on the part of States and their leaders, and on the erosion of their reluctance by the "well-intentioned", through a firm and persistent game of patience. – At the condition of course that we will be given the time!

In the international field, in front of the obvious difficulty of making rapid, significant progress of the System in the political area, it seems advisable to favor the development of its many branches that deal with specific tasks, especially in the social and humanitarian fields. In fact, while member states appear to be less reluctant to delegate, in abstract and step by step, supranational roles to such organizations, it is a fact that these, somehow as apprentice sorcerers, tend gradually to assume a more and more independent – and eventually political – role, based especially on the growing support and pressure exerted by the civil society.

Human rights deserve a particular mention when dealing with human solidarity, as it is in their field that the more significant progresses have been made especially thanks to the Universal Declaration of Human Rights and the large body of conventions into which it developed. All norms consistently directing the world toward humanism and tolerance. We must also recognize that it is in the sphere of human rights that the sovereignty shield has shown the less resistance.

Having said that, we must unfortunately also recognize that genuine practical acceptance and implementation of many human rights norms is lagging. For instance discrimination on the bases of sex, creed, race or ethnicity is still common as we are often dealing with deeply engrained cultural patterns. While the transposition of subscribed international norms into the national spheres is painfully slow.

Particularly arduous it will be to obtain a sincere commitment by the multinational companies, focused as they are on the quest of larger and easier profits in the shortest possible time. Especially in the present stage of a globalization which, so far, has focused more on the rights of corporations rather than on their responsibilities while, in addition, the political and economical components of globalization move at such different pace.

It is therefore especially in the adoption on the part of its main protagonists, even if half heartedly, of a more far-sighted policy, that lays the hope of a more promising evolution.

On the other hand, under the current circumstances, in the political field the more promising approach resides in prevention: in other words in the ability to tackle potential crises as precociously as possible.

We have in fact under our eyes daily examples of how difficult it is to resolve conflicts already underway, especially if long standing.

The crisis – different in nature, but all equally resilient – I have witnessed in Congo, Somalia, Syria and Palestine, make me, if not skeptical, certainly very prudent in believing in an early overcoming of conflicts that have turned chronic.

In general the world situation has been made more complex and dangerous by the gradual expansion within States of internal conflicts that, as such, tend to short-circuit the internal and the international Institutions and adopt means of struggle more insidious and difficult to control. In fact the reluctance, more conceptual than political, to open a dialog and a negotiation with entities deprived of international personality, tends to make inacceptable (on both sides) the adoption of rules of behavior consenting progress towards the overcoming of conflicts.

But even in the international conflicts a significant step could be made with the acceptance of a wider set of rules of behavior that – even if morally repugnant – in the first place would limit the kind of weapons admissible in case of war. Even in its imperfection, such an approach would favor progress towards a growing sense of collective responsibility, and therefore of solidarity, diminishing the solitude in which are conducted the efforts both of generous individuals (Mother Teresa of Culcutta; The Mahatma Gandhi; and so on ...) and of several multilateral as well as governmental and nongovernmental organizations.

It seems therefore that a good start would consist in intervening with the most possible anticipation to eliminate the predictable causes of conflict (border disputes; basic utilities; religious, ethnic and tribal disputes; and so on ...) and by gradually reducing the right of veto now prevailing in multilateral organizations in favor of a more democratic practice.

Alas, we know how arduous is the way towards the acceptance of such an attitude, as demonstrated by so many examples; for instance by what is happening within the European Union where, against any obvious logic, the prevailing tendency is that of a shortsighted particularism and attachment to individual, long over passed roles that do not take into account the evolution of the new world.

Anyway, never was more appropriate the famous motto reading "it is not necessary to hope for undertaking", especially in the absence of credible alternatives.

Dealing with human solidarity at the individual level is at the same time simpler and more difficult in so far from immemorial time those in power have imposed on their subjects, in a more or less humane and democratic manner, rules of cohabitation, while more challenging remains to obtain a solidary behavior based on a spontaneous attitude of individuals.

When analyzing human solidarity unavoidably special attention must be devoted to religion as possibly the first phenomenon deeply influencing human behavior, even if in so doing one risks to touch very sensitive cords. As matter of fact this very powerful sentiment – or should one say "this need and necessity" – assimilates since time in memorial all humans on the base, after all, of very similar principles while at the same time inspiring both the most solidary and generous behaviors, as well as the most intolerant and aggressive ones. As such, it epitomizes the contradiction from which we have developed our analyses. Therefore, it is probably in the difficult task of overcoming this basic ambivalence that resides the first fundamental step towards improving human solidarity. This uphill undertaking would imply, in the first place, the accepting (and preaching!) on the part of religious leaders, of the principle that all religions, from the most primitive to the loftiest and most sophisticated ones, pursue the very same finalities. And in the first place that of obviating to the most unbearable curs of man: that of not finding answers to very many of the questions that he has become able to put himself. In other words that would mean simply understanding and accepting the old saying according to which the summit of a mountain can be reached from all its different sides. While accepting this principle would not require being less committed and diligent in following the dictates of the faith of one's culture or choice, but at the same time would imply being tolerant towards those of the others.

To conclude on a lighter note, I will refer to Wilder Penfield's theory according to which our mind contains two *homunculi*: one motorial and one sensorial. Referring to the assumption from which I started, I suggest to amend Penfield's theory assigning to the first homunculus the instinctive/emotional functions and to the other the rational ones. In other words, to recognize that our mind is the perpetual battlefield of our personal, inseparable Doctor Jekyll and Mr. Hide.

Concept that Jawaharlal Nehru, with his peerless elegance put as follows: "Whatever Gods there be, there is something godlike in man, as there is also something of the devil in man.

All this will have to be taken into account by the men and women of good will in their efforts to promote human solidarity.

List of contributors

Dr. ANINDITA N. BALSLEV is the initiator of the program entitled 'cross-cultural conversation' (CCC). With educational and professional experience in India, France, USA and Denmark, she works in the areas of both Indian and Western philosophy. She was formerly Associate Research Professor at the Department of Philosophy at the University of Copenhagen. She has been Visiting professor at Aarhus University and various other universities in India and in USA. She has served on the Advisory board of the American Association for the Advancement of Science (DOSER) and has been invited speaker at several science-religion programs organized by the Smithsonian Institution, Institute for Religion in the Age of Science, Georgetown University and AAAS. She has published many papers in professional journals and is the author of *A Study of Time in Indian Philosophy* (Germany 1983/India 1999); *Cultural Otherness: Correspondence with Richard Rorty* (USA, 1999). She is also the co-editor of *Religion and Time* (The Netherlands, 1993), and the editor of *Cross-Cultural Conversation* (USA, 1996).

PROF. DR. REINHOLD BERNHARDT is Professor of Systematic Theology / Dogmatics at the University of Basel (Switzerland). He has his doctorate in theology from the University of Heidelberg. He has travelled widely and his professional academic experience includes various universities in Germany, Switzerland and the US. He has published more than 50 articles on various subjects in books and periodicals and is the author of a number of books, including: *Was heißt Handeln Gottes? Eine Rekonstruktion der Lehre von der Vorsehung*, Gütersloh 1999; *Ende des Dialogs? Die Begegnung der Religionen und ihre theologische Reflexion*, Zürich 2006; as editor: *Kriterien religiöser Urteilsbildung* (Beiträge zu einer Theologie der Religionen 1), Zürich 2005.

Rabbi Bob Carrol is a graduate of Brandeis, University, where he studied Judaic Studies and Philosophy, and received both a Masters Degree in Jewish Philosophy as well as Rabbinic Ordination from Yeshiva University in New York. He has also completed doctoral coursework in Jewish and Islamic Mysticism at New York University, spent a number of years studying in Israeli Yeshivot, and has spent considerable time as well in the study of Native American religious beliefs and practices. He currently lives in Jerusalem, Israel, where he is the Director of Development and Communications for the Interfaith Encounter Association, frequently teaches at interfaith dialog sessions and retreats, and also volunteers as a soldier in an anti-terrorist unit of the Israel Border Guard.

Prof. Lokesh Chandra is a renowned scholar of Tibetan, Mongolian and Sino-Japanese Buddhism. He has to his credit 581 works and text-editions. Among them are his classics like his *Tibetan-Sanskrit-Dictionary, Materials for a History of Tibetan Literature, Mongolian Kanjus* in 108 volumes and the *Dictionary of Buddhist Iconography* in 15 volumes. He was nominated to the Parliament 1974–80 and 1980–86. He has been Vice President of ICCR and Chairman of ICHR. Presently, he is Director of the International Academy of Indian Culture.

Dr. Homi Dhalla was awarded the M.A. degree by Harvard University in Near Eastern Languages and Literatures and the Ph.D. degree from Mumbai University from the Department of Avesta-Pahlavi. He taught as Assistent Professor at the Asia institute, Shiraz University, Iran for two years. He has been conducting research in Zoroastrian Studies and Parsi History for many years. He has represented the Parsi community at various international conferenes focusing on the issues of peace, ecology, human rights, interreligious dialogue, etc. For his contribution to the interfaith movement over two decades, he was awarded "The Mother Teresa National Award for Interfaith Harmony" in April 2007.

Geshe Lakh Dor has served as translator to His Holiness the Dalai Lama for 16 years and had travelled with him to several countries. He received his Master in English from Punjab University, Chandigarth, his Geshe Degree (Doctor in Divinity) from Drepung Loseling Monastic University in South India, MPhil in Buddhist Philosophy from Delhi University. He is presently

the Director of the Library of Tibetan Works and Archives in Dharam-
sala, a trustee of the Foundation for Universal Responsibility, established
by His Holiness the Dalai Lama, Honorary Professor of the University of
British Columbia, Vancouver, Honorary Professor in the Department of
Psychology, University of Delhi. He is also co-translator and co-producer
of numerous books and articles.

ASHGAR ALI ENGINEER has been nominated as member of National Integration Council in the year 2005 by Prime Minister of India. He is the
Chairman of the Centre for Study of Society and Secularism, Mumbai and
is also Director of the Institute of Islamic Studies, Mumbai. He has received
many awards, such as the Right Livelihood Honorary Award (also called
the Alternate Nobel Award) for vision and work, Stockholm, Sweden, 2004;
the National Communal Award, 1997 presented by Home Ministry, Govt.
of Indi; Honorary degree of D.Litt. by University of Calcutta, 1993; Honorary degree of D.Litt. by Jamia Hamdard, Islamic University, New Delhi,
2005; Honorary degree of D.Litt. by Jamia Millia Islamia Central University, New Delhi, 2008. He has published 62 books on Islam, Problems of
Muslims, Muslim Women's rights, Communal and Ethnic Problem in India, South Asia and Islamic States. He also publishes a fortnightly *Secular
Perspectives* and monthly *Islam and Modern Age*.

REVD. DR. DIRK EVERS is Associate Professor for Systematic Theology at
Tübingen University, Germany. He studied Protestant theology at the Universities of Münster and Tübingen (Germany) and at the Tamilnadu Theological Seminary, Madurai (South India) from 1983–1989. He is an ordained
minister of the Lutheran Church. From 1994–2005 he worked as assistant
lecturer in Systematic Theology at Tübingen University (chair of Eberhard
Jüngel). In 1999 he received his doctorate in theology with a thesis on *Space
– Matter – Time. Christian theology of creation in dialogue with scientific
cosmology* which won the ESSSAT-prize 2002 of the European Society for
the Study of Science and Theology. He completed his postdoctoral studies (Habilitation) with a work on *God and possible worlds. Studies in the
logic of theological discourse on possibility*. Since 2005 he is working as Director of Studies at the FORUM SCIENTIARUM of Tuebingen University,
Germany. He has published numerous articles in systematic theology and

science and religion and lectured widely in that field, mainly in Germany and Switzerland.

AMBASSADOR GIORGIO GIACOMELLI was born in Milano, Italy. He holds a master's degree in law from the University of Padua. He also studied at Cambridge University (UK) and at the Geneva's Institute of Higher International Studies. He joined the Italian diplomatic corps in 1956 and served in Madrid, Paris, Leopoldville (now Kinshasa), New Delhi and was Italy's Ambassador to Somalia and Syria. Since December 1999 until March 2001, Mr Giacomelli was appointed, by the Commission of the United Nations for Human Rights, at the rank of Special Reporter for human rights in the Palestinian occupied territories since 1967. In July 2002 did Ambassador Giacomelli take the chairmanship of HYDROAID, a non-profit association focused on training in water resource management for the developing countries. In 2006, Secretary General Kofi Annan appointed Ambassador Giacomelli as Member of the UN Advisory Board on Water and Sanitation. Mr. Giacomelli is a recipient of a number of awards and decorations, including the Silver Medal for Civil Bravery of Italy, the Légion d' honneur of France and the Knight in the Order of Merit of Italy.

DR. ALON GOSHEN-GOTTSTEIN has been director of the Elijah Interfaith Institute and lecturer and director of the Center for the Study of Rabbinic Thought, Beit Morasha College, both in Jerusalem, since 1997. He has also lectured at the Ratisbonne Pontifical Institute in Jerusalem, 1997–2001; the School of Overseas Students, Tel Aviv University, 1997–99; the Schehter Institute of Jewish Studies, 1996–98; the Dept. of Jewish History, Track for Jewish Thought, at both Haifa and Ben Gurion universities, 1996; and guest lectured at the University of Uppsala, 1996–97. He was a teaching assistant and lecturer in the Dept. of Jewish Philosophy at Tel Aviv University, 1991–95. Ordained a rabbi in 1977, he holds a B.A. from Hebrew University of Jerusalem, where he did a preparatory year for a direct doctoral program. In 1982, he did a year of research on the New Testament and ancient religions at Harvard Divinity School. He received his Ph.D. from Hebrew University of Jerusalem in 1986. From 1989 to 1999, he was a member of the Shalom Hartman Institute for Advanced Studies, Jerusalem. Stanford University Press published his *The Sinner and the Amnesiac: The Rabbinic Invention of Elisha ben Abuya and Eleazar ben Arach* in 2000, and his *Israel in God's Presence: An Introduction to Judaism for the Christian Student* is forthcoming from Hendrickson Press. His nearly three dozen articles have appeared in edited collections and in such scholarly journals as Harvard Theological Review, Journal for the Study of Judaism, Journal of Literature and Theology, Journal of Jewish Thought and Philosophy, Ecumenism, and Studies in Interreligious Dialogue.

PROF. SAMDHONG RINPOCHE was born in Tibet, he started his religious training at Drepung Monastry in Lhasa and completed his middle school of the Madhyamika School of Buddhism at the age of 12. From October 1961, he served as the religious teacher of Tibetan School in Shimla, and later became the acting principal of Shimla Tibetan School in 1963. He returned to religious teaching, at Darjeeling Tibetan School, the following year. He returned to religious teaching, at Darjeeling Tibetan School, the following year. From 1965 to 1970, the Samdhong Rinpoche was the Principal of Dalhousie Tibetan School. He received his Lharampa Degree in the year 1968 and Ngagrimpa Degree in 1969. From 1971 to 1988 he was the Principal of the Central Institute of Higher Tibetan Studies (CIHTS, Varanasi). From 1988 to 2001 he worked as the Director of CIHTS. In 1990, he became a member of the Drafting Committee of the Constitution of the Future Polity of Tibet and Law for the exiled Tibetans. From 1991 to 1995 he was specially appointed by the 14th Dalai Lama as one of the deputies of the Parliament of the Central Tibetan Administration and later was unanimously elected as its Chairman. From 1996 to 2001 he was elected member of the Parliament from Kham province and also its Chairman.

PROF. DR. VEMPATI KUTUMBA SASTRY was born in 1950 at Gudlavalleru, Krishna District, Andhra Pradesh, and had his Rgveda adhyayana at Tirupati; he qualified Vidyapravina (M.A.) from Andhra University, Waltair, and Siromani (M.A.) from the University of Madras. He received Vidyavaridhi (Ph.D.) degree from the Rashtriya Sanskrit Sansthan, New Delhi, and has also qualified in M.A. (Philosophy) and P.G. Diploma in Yoga from Sri Venkateswara University, Tirupati. He worked as a Lecturer in Sri Narasimha Samskrit College, Chittiguduru, Krishna District, Andhra Pradesh, and in the Rashtriya Sanskrit Sansthan, New Delhi. He next held the position of Professor and Head of the Department of Sanskrit, Pondicherry University from 1990 until 2004. He became Director of the Rashtriya Sanskrit

Sansthan in 1999 and then in 2003 its Vice Chancellor. He is now Vice-Chancellor of Sampurnanand Sanskrit University, Varanasi and President of the International Association for Sanskrit Studies. His specialisations are in Advaita Vedanta, the Darsanas, Poetics, Sanskrit Literature and Spoken Sanskrit. He has written six books and more than 30 papers, published in various journals.

DR. KARAN SINGH is the Chairman of the Auroville Foundation, President of the Indian Council for Cultural Relations, Chancellor of the Jawaharlal University and a member of Parliament with the personal rank of Central Cabinet Minister. For many years he has been Chancellor of Jammu and Kashmir University as well as of the Benares Hindu University. He has received many awards of distinction. He is member of the prestigious Club of Rome and Club of Budapest. He has written a number of books. His autobiography entitled *As I see it* and his *Essays on Hinduism* have been widely acclaimed.

PROF. M.S. SWAMINATHAN is an Indian agriculture scientist, born 1925 in Kumbakonam, Tamilnadu. A plant geneticist by training, Prof. Swaminathan is known as the "Father of the Green Revolution in India" for introducing and further developing high-yielding varieties of wheat in India. He advocates a sustainable agriculture leading to an ever-green revolution which makes him an acknowledged leader in the field of sustainable food security. The International Association of Women and Development conferred on him the first international award for significant contributions to promoting the knowledge, skill, and technological empowerment of women in agriculture and for his pioneering role in mainstreaming gender considerations in agriculture and rural development. He is founder and Chairman of the MS Swaminathan Research Foundation. He was Chairman of the UN Science Advisory Committee set up in 1980 to take follow-up action on the Vienna Plan of Action. He has also served as Independent Chairman of the FAO Council and President of the International Union for the Conservation of Nature and Natural Resources. Professor Swaminathan was awarded the Ramon Magsaysay Award for Community Leadership in 1971, the Albert Einstein World Science Award in 1986, and the first World Food Prize in 1987. Professor Swaminathan is a Fellow of many of the leading scientific academies of India and the world, including the

Royal Society of London and the U S National Academy of Sciences. He has received 58 honorary doctorate degrees from universities around the world. He currently holds the UNESCO Chair in Ecotechnology at the M S Swaminathan Research Foundation in Chennai (Madras), India.

AMBASSADOR ROBERTO TOSCANO is an Italian diplomat, currently ambassador in India. Before India, he has served in Chile, the Soviet Union, Spain, the US, Geneva (UN) and Iran. He was a visiting professor of International Relations in the Department of Political Science at LUISS University in Rome from 2000–2003. He holds a Law Degree from the University of Parma, Italy, and an M.A. in International Relations from John Hopkins University (School of Advanced International Studies). He is the author of books and articles an ethics and international relations, human rights and conflict prevention. Recently a book he wrote with Ramin Jahanbegloo was published with the title *Beyond Violence. Principles for an Open Century.*

The publication "Compassion in the World's Religions and Human Solidarity" is funded by

UDO KELLER STIFTUNG
FORUM HUMANUM

In a time of increasing access by technology and economy to mankind, the Foundation would like to remind people of the meaning of the spiritual and religious legacy of human world cultures. It assumes that the future development of mankind will depend decisively on whether we are successful in making the rich potential of these traditions beneficial for the future. To this end, the Udo Keller Foundation Forum Humanum pleads for a revival of the question about the meaning of human life in line with the conditions of the 21st century.

For further information about the Udo Keller Foundation, please visit **www.forum-humanum.org**.

Religionswissenschaft: Forschung und Wissenschaft

Klaus Bayer
Religiöse Sprache
Thesen zur Einführung
Religiöse Texte sind meist in besonderer Weise poetisch gestaltet; zudem sind ihre Semantik, Metaphorik und Argumentation oft überraschend. Allerdings finden sich jene Merkmale, die auf den ersten Blick Besonderheiten religiöser Sprache zu sein scheinen, auch in profanen Texten etwa der Politik, des Sports oder der Popkultur. Man darf sich deshalb religiösen Sprachgebrauch nicht als eine Insel der Irrationalität in einem Meer profaner Rationalität vorstellen: Die Unzulänglichkeiten menschlicher Weltbildkonstruktion treten in religiösen Texten allenfalls hier und da besonders deutlich zutage.
Das Buch bietet Religionswissenschaftlern, Sprach- und Literaturwissenschaftlern – insbesondere auch zukünftigen Lehrern – einen Schlüssel zum Verständnis religiöser Sprache sowie einen Einblick in religiöse Funktionen profaner Texte.
Bd. 2, 2., überarb. Aufl 2009, 128 S., 9,90 €, br.,
ISBN 9782 3-8258-8061-3

Reto Luzius Fetz
Shri Ramana Maharshi: Vom Ich zum Selbst
Hinduistische Mystik im westlichen Vergleich
Bd. 3, 2006, 200 S., 19,90 €, br., ISBN 3-8258-9662-5

Hannelore Winkler
Sündflut, entschlüsselt aus Lehrtexten seit dem 2. Jahrtausend v. Chr.
Textsammlung: Sumer, Altbabylonien, Judäa-Israel, Griechenland, Römisches Reich und Kaiserreich Österreich 19. Jh.
Flutberichte haben sich weltweit erhalten. Sie zählen zum frühesten Traditionsgut aller Nationen. Es ist richtig, daß zu einem bestimmten Zeitpunkt größere Landpartien tatsächlich unter Wasser standen. Wir haben es keineswegs mit mythischen Berichten zu tun, wie oft gesagt wird. Sondern umgekehrt, wir sehen, daß gleichartiges Wissen zu einem Schöpfergott, zur Herkunft der Menschen und Gerichte Gottes bei Fehlverhalten, seit mehreren tausend Jahren in allen Kulturen verbreitet gewesen waren. Ganz gleich wo die Menschen lebten, mit dem Thema Sündflut waren alle Personen vor uns durch Lehrtexte vertraut.
Bd. 4, 2008, 448 S., 69,90 €, br., ISBN 978-3-8258-0397-1

Benedikt Rothöhler, Alexander Manisali (Hg.)

Mythos & Ritual

Festschrift für Jan Assmann zum 70. Geburtstag

Religionswissenschaft: Forschung und Wissenschaft

LIT

Benedikt Rothöhler;
Alexander Manisali (Hg.)
Mythos & Ritual
Festschrift für Jan Assmann zum 70. Geburtstag
Die vorliegende Festschrift *Mythos & Ritual* ehrt den Ägyptologen Jan Assmann. Die Vielfalt von dessen Beiträgen zu diesen für das pharaonische Ägypten so wichtigen Bereichen spiegelt sich in den Artikeln aus dem Kollegen- und Schülerkreis wider: Die Themen reichen von der Tempeldekoration über das Verhältnis von Text und Bild in Ritualtexten bis zur Musik im Kult. Mit einem Beitrag zur Diskussion um den zeitgenössischen Gehalt religiöser Traditionen reicht das zeitliche Spektrum über die griechisch-römische Zeit Ägyptens hinaus. Mit Beiträgen u. a. von Terence DuQuesne, Louise Gestermann, Friedhelm Hoffmann, Ulrich Luft, Colleen Manassa, Manfred Oeming, Joachim Quack, Thomas Schneider, Anthony Spalinger, Michael Welker und Jürgen Zeidler.
Bd. 5, 2008, 336 S., 39,90 €, br., ISBN 978-3-8258-1145-7

LIT Verlag Berlin – Münster – Wien – Zürich – London
Auslieferung Deutschland / Österreich / Schweiz: siehe Impressumsseite

Religionen in der pluralen Welt

Religionswissenschaftliche Studien zum Transfer zwischen den Religionen
hrsg. von Prof. Dr. Dr. Christoph Auffarth (Universität Bremen), Prof. Dr. Günter Kehrer (Universität Tübingen) und Prof. Dr. Michael Zank (Universität Boston)
Schriftleitung Oliver Grasmück

Christoph Auffarth
Religiöser Pluralismus im Mittelalter?
Besichtigung einer Epoche der Europäischen Religionsgeschichte. Mit Beiträgen von Ulrich Berner, Winfried Frey, Kocku von Stuckrad und Nicole Zeddies
„Religiöser Pluralismus im Mittelalter" – das scheint nur auf den ersten Blick befremdlich. Ist doch bis heute das Bild mittelalterlicher Religiosität geprägt durch die seit der Romantik vorherrschende Vorstellung einer katholisch-lateinischen Einheitskultur. Im vorliegenden Auftaktband der Reihe „Religionen in der pluralen Welt" rücken der Religionswissenschafler Christoph Auffarth und seine Mitautoren dagegen gerade die religiöse Vielfalt des Mittelalters in den Mittelpunkt und schaffen so überraschende neue Einblicke in eine bis heute wirkmächtige Epoche Europäischer Religionsgeschichte.
Bd. 1, 2007, 176 S., 19,90 €, br., ISBN 978-3-8258-8631-8

Alexander Kenneth Nagel
Charitable Choice – Religiöse Institutionalisierung im öffentlichen Raum
Religion und Sozialpolitik in den USA
Bd. 4, 2006, 200 S., 19,90 €, br., ISBN 3-8258-8955-6

Thorsten Laue
Kundalini Yoga, Yogi Tee und das Wassermannzeitalter
Religionswissenschaftliche Einblicke in die Healthy, Happy, Holy Organization (3HO) des Yogi Bhajan
Yogi Bhajan (1929–2004) gründete 1969 die Healthy, Happy, Holy Organization (3HO), die in den USA zugleich als Sikh Dharma Bekanntheit erlangte. Wer ist der Mann hinter „Yogi Tee", dem der amerikanische Kongress die gleiche Ehrung zuteil werden ließ wie Mutter Theresa, Martin Luther King und Papst Johannes Paul II? Seit ihrer Entstehung vor 30 Jahren wird die 3H Organisation Deutschland e.V. – Fach- und Ausbildungsverband für Kundalini Yoga – zum ersten Mal wissenschaftlich dargestellt. Abbildungen und eine Mantra-Sammlung ergänzen den Einblick in den Lebensstil des „Wassermannzeitalters".
Bd. 5, 2007, 104 S., 14,90 €, br., ISBN 978-3-8258-0140-3

Manfred Hutter (Hg.)
Religionswissenschaft im Kontext der Asienwissenschaften
99 Jahre religionswissenschaftliche Lehre und Forschung in Bonn
Seit 1910 ist an der Universität Bonn das Fach Vergleichende Religionswissenschaft etabliert, das in enger Wechselwirkung zu den Asienwissenschaften steht. Professor(inn)en verschiedener Universitäten als Absolventen des Religionswissenschaftlichen Seminars und aktuelle Mitarbeiter(innen) sind die Autor(inn)en dieses Bandes. Mit Beiträgen zu Methoden- und Theoriefragen, Analysen von Teilen des Œuvres der in Bonn tätigen Professoren Carl Clemen († 1940), Gustav Mensching († 1978) und Hans-Joachim Klimkeit († 1999) und mit religionshistorischen Detailstudien geben sie Einblick in die Bonner Ausrichtung des Faches.
Bd. 8, 2009, 288 S., 34,90 €, br., ISBN 978-3-643-10332-1

LIT Verlag Berlin – Münster – Wien – Zürich – London

Auslieferung Deutschland / Österreich / Schweiz: siehe Impressumsseite

Religiösität – Spiritualität – Gesundheit

hrsg. von Prof. Dr. Arndt Büssing (Witten/Herdecke), Prof. Dr. Harold G. Koenig (Durham, USA) und Prof. Dr. Günter Riße (Vallendar)

Hildegard Strickerschmidt
Geerdete Spiritualität bei Hildegard von Bingen
Neue Zugänge zu ihrer Heilkunde
Hildegard von Bingen, über die Grenzen Europas hinaus bekannte Heilkundige und Mystikerin des 12. Jahrhunderts, gilt als erste deutsche Verfasserin eines medizinischen Werkes. Heil sein bedeutet ihr mehr als ein Zustand von Beschwerdefreiheit, der heute mit Gesundheit umschrieben wird. Aus ihrer umfassenden Schau von Kosmos, Mensch und Gott heraus bietet sie in überzeitlicher Gültigkeit Wege zu Heilung und Heil an. Mit diesem Buch werden die verschiedenen Bereiche ihrer Heilkunde vorgestellt und für den heutigen Menschen zugänglich gemacht.
Bd. 1, 2007, 240 S., 19,90 €, br., ISBN 3-8258-9739-7

Martin Pott; Ulrich Roth
Würde als Maß
Psychiatrieseelsorge als sozialpsychiatrisches Handeln
Die Psychiatrielandschaft verändert sich massiv. Die Verweildauer im stationären Bereich hat sich stark verkürzt. „Ambulant vor stationär" heißt das neue Prinzip. Behandlung und Begleitung psychisch kranker Menschen sollen möglichst gemeindenah erfolgen. Psychiatrieseelsorge muss diese Entwicklung ernst nehmen. Sie muss ihren stationären Ansatz weiten und ihrerseits ambulant, gemeindenah und vernetzt agieren. Seelsorge wird damit Teil des gemeindepsychiatrischen Verbunds. Im Großraum Aachen hat sich die Psychiatrieseelsorge dieser Herausforderung gestellt. Der vorliegende Band begründet die neue Praxis theologisch wie sozialpsychiatrisch und berichtet von konkreten Schritten in seelsorglichem „Neuland".
Bd. 3, 2007, 128 S., 14,90 €, br., ISBN 978-3-8258-9216-6

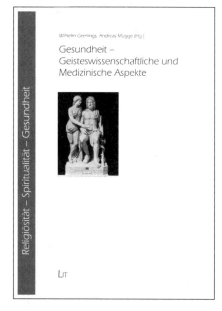

Wilhelm Geerlings; Andreas Mügge (Hg.)
Gesundheit – Geisteswissenschaftliche und Medizinische Aspekte
Die Sorge um die eigene Gesundheit ist ein Urphänomen der Menschheit. Der Sammelband fasst Referate zusammen, die im Rahmen einer Ringvorlesung Gesundheit – geisteswissenschaftliche und medizinische Aspekte an der Ruhr-Universität Bochum im Jahr 2006/2007 abgehalten wurden. Die Beiträge spannen einen Bogen von antiken Patientenzeugnissen über die Angst um die eigene Gesundheit bis hin zu den Grenzen des heute medizinisch Machbaren.
Bd. 4, 2009, 288 S., 29,90 €, gb., ISBN 978-3-643-10026-9

LIT Verlag Berlin – Münster – Wien – Zürich – London
Auslieferung Deutschland / Österreich / Schweiz: siehe Impressumsseite

Religiöse Gegenwart Asiens / Studies in Modern Asian Religions
edited by Michael Pye and Monika Schrimpf

Michael Pye; Katja Triplett
Streben nach Glück
Schicksalsdeutung und Lebensgestaltung in japanischen Religionen. Mit Beiträgen von Monika Schrimpf
Bd. 1, 2007, 304 S., 29,90 €, br., ISBN 978-3-8258-7989-1

Katja Triplett
Menschenopfer und Selbstopfer in den japanischen Legenden
Das Frankfurter Manuskript der Matsura Sayohime-Legende
Bd. 2, 2005, 392 S., 29,90 €, br., ISBN 3-8258-7990-9

Edith Franke; Michael Pye (Hg.)
Religionen Nebeneinander
Modelle religiöser Vielfalt in Ost- und Süd-ostasien
Bd. 3, 2006, 152 S., 24,90 €, br., ISBN 3-8258-8411-2

Simone Heidegger
Buddhismus, Geschlechterverhältnis und Diskriminierung
Die gegenwärtige Diskussion im Shin-Buddhismus Japans
Bd. 4, 2006, 504 S., 39,90 €, br., ISBN 3-8258-8771-5

Ugo Dessì
Ethics and Society in Contemporary Shin Buddhism
Bd. 5, 2007, 272 S., 39,90 €, br., ISBN 978-3-8258-0815-0

Interreligious Studies
edited by Prof. Dr. Frans Wijsen and Dr. Jorge E. Castillo Guerra (Radboud University, Nijmegen)

José M. Vigil; Luiza Tomita;
Marcello Barros (Eds.)
Along the Many Paths of God
Foreword: Pedro Casadáliga
Latin American theology is associated with libe-ration, basic Christian communities, primacy of praxis and option for the poor. The present volume shows that Latin American theologians added new themes to the previous ones: religious pluralism, inter-religious dialogue and macro-ecumenism. It is the fruti of a programme of the Theological Com-mission of the Ecumenical Association of Third

World Theologians (EATWOT) in Latin America, to work out a liberating theology of religions.
Bd. 1, 2008, 288 S., 29,90 €, br., ISBN 978-3-8258-1520-2

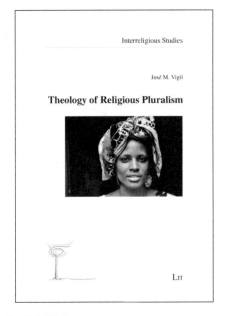

José M. Vigil
Theology of Religious Pluralism
This book offers a theology of religious pluralism. It was conceived and developed in Latin America from the perspective of liberation theology. One of the issues at play in the liberation of humanity is the world's ability to accept religious pluralism, and Latin American theology does not want to be silent on this topic. Born out of Latin American spirituality, this theology of religious pluralism is a liberating theology. It may be the first Latin American book that seeks to express something complete and systematic on this topic from the perspective of this continent and that of liberation theology.
Bd. 2, 2008, 360 S., 34,90 €, br., ISBN 978-3-8258-1519-6

LIT Verlag Berlin – Münster – Wien – Zürich – London
Auslieferung Deutschland / Österreich / Schweiz: siehe Impressumsseite